the Naked Kitchen

Because everything tastes better naked.

Veggie Burger Book

Delicious Plant-Based Burgers, Fries, Sides, and More

Sarah Davies & Kristy Taylor

LYONS PRESS
Guilford, Connecticut
An imprint of Globe Pequot Press

Photos by Sarah Davies
Text design: Sheryl P. Kober
Project editor: Julie Marsh
Layout artist: Melissa Evarts

Library of Congress Cataloging-in-Publication Data is available on file.

ISBN 978-0-7627-9329-7

Printed in the United States of America
10 9 8 7 6 5 4 3 2 1

To my husband—my soul mate and my biggest supporter. To my children, Caleb, Keegan, and Madelyn, who bring the most joy to my life. And, of course, to my mother—my cooking partner in crime and best friend. I can't imagine doing this with anyone else! —Sarah

My part in this book is dedicated to my daughter, Sarah, who has allowed me to share in the joy of this culinary journey. —Kristy

Contents

Vegetable Burgers

Burger Buns

Condiments and Toppings

Sides and Salads

Beyond Burgers

Introduction

Throughout my youth and into my twenties, I never worried about what I ate or how it impacted my health. It wasn't until I became a wife—and, more important, a mother—that I realized if I wanted to enjoy a long and healthy life with my family, I would have to start taking care of myself.

When I started researching different types of food and their effects on our bodies, I soon discovered the beauty of a whole-foods, plant-based diet. Many people assume the term is just a fancy way of saying vegan or vegetarian, but this is not at all the case. So what exactly is a whole-foods, plant-based diet? In the simplest terms, it is a diet that involves eating plants. It focuses on organic vegetables, fruits, grains, and legumes and eliminates artificially processed and refined foods, meat, dairy, and eggs. It's the elimination of processed and refined foods that sets a plant-based diet apart from other diets and lifestyles. For example, many highly processed foods qualify as vegan simply because they contain no meat or animal products. An Oreo cookie is vegan for this very reason, yet most of us would agree that it is not a healthy food choice. If you read the ingredients on a package of Oreo cookies, you will see how unhealthy each and every ingredient is! Sometimes even products that are marketed as "health foods," including most imitation meats, are loaded with refined sugars, artificial ingredients, and added chemicals and preservatives that belong in a laboratory, not on your plate.

It was during this journey into a plant-based diet that The Naked Kitchen was born. When I started out, I was by no means skilled in the kitchen. I just wanted people to see that eating healthy didn't have to be boring or taste bad. Many of the unhealthy foods that people like to consume can easily be recreated to be not only nutritious and vastly better for their health and well-being, but every bit as flavorful and enjoyable, too. Fortunately for me, my mother, Kristy, had already been eating a healthy, mostly plant-based diet for years, so I peppered her with questions and eventually she became my brilliant cooking partner. Together, we worked to design and develop The Naked Kitchen.

Today, The Naked Kitchen is a website where health-conscious eaters of every background can come together to find nutritious, sustainable, and, most importantly, amazingly delicious recipes. Our goal is not to establish labels or convert people to any dietary dogma, but to encourage everyone—from meat eaters to vegetarian to vegans—to create wonderful meals that *all* their friends and family members will love. We believe in a down-to-earth, hands-on approach to everyday cooking, which is why we are drawn to comfort foods. And what could be more comforting than a yummy burger?

One of the first plant-based meals I created for my family was a basic bean burger. We paired it with a side of baked sweet potato fries, and it was so delicious that we never looked back. When Kristy and I were discussing a theme for this cookbook, I kept going back to that simple, easy meal I first created and how effortless it made the transition from a meat-based diet to a plant-based one. We thought how great it would be to provide people with a wide variety of tasty burgers that they can quickly whip up for themselves and their families to enjoy. Some of our most popular recipes on The Naked Kitchen website are traditional, family-friendly dishes. Our readers constantly ask us for easy meals that are hearty and filling. Through our cooking classes, social media, and website, The Naked Kitchen community has provided us with tremendous support and invaluable feedback, which we have poured lovingly into every page of this cookbook.

May these recipes bring you health and happiness as you feed yourself and those you love with wholesome, delicious plant-based creations!

—*Sarah Davies*
Oceanside, CA

THE BASICS

Going Organic

The term "organic" has become a marketing buzzword, but what exactly does it mean and why is it important to you? Simply stated, organic produce and other ingredients are grown without the use of pesticides, synthetic fertilizers, sewage sludge, genetically modified organisms (GMOs), or ionizing radiation. Organic foods provide us with the safest, healthiest foods for our bodies. The pesticides and chemicals that are used on conventional food products are not meant to be in our bodies. Numerous studies have linked their use to cancer and other degenerative diseases, as well as autism.

One of the most widely used pesticides is Monsanto's Roundup, which is available in different varieties at your local lawn and garden stores. When you sit down to eat tonight, ask yourself, would you ever think about spraying your dinner with Roundup? Of course not! It's poison, after all. Just read the label—it's labeled as hazardous with a warning to "Keep away from food, drink and animal feeding stuffs." Yet this is exactly what is sprayed on our foods, and it doesn't wash off with water either.

Buying organic food products also protects you from consuming GMOs, which are plants or animals created through the gene-splicing techniques of biotechnology. Most developed nations do not consider GMOs to be safe. In nearly fifty countries around the world, including Australia, Japan, and all of the countries in the European Union, there are significant restrictions or outright bans on the production and sale of GMOs. In the United States, the government has approved GMOs based on studies conducted by the same corporations that created them and profit from their sale. Increasingly, Americans are taking matters into their own hands and choosing to opt out of the GMO experiment.

The organic food industry is now a billion-dollar industry and supermarkets all over the nation are stocking their shelves with organic produce and products. When shopping for organic produce make sure to check the label. Organic produce labels will have a five-digit code that begins with the number 9. For packaged food items look for labels that say "100% Organic" or "USDA Organic." These labels will ensure that the items you are buying are made with at least 95 percent organic ingredients.

When buying organic produce, it's always best to buy items that are in season. Not only will the produce be fresher, it will also help to save you money. Farmers' markets and co-ops are also great places to buy inexpensive organic produce and specialty items. You'll not only be buying fresh, local foods, but you'll be helping to support your local farmers. Seeking out your local community-supported agriculture network (CSA) is also a wonderful way to get fresh, local, organic produce. Check around in your area for a farmers' market or CSA and enjoy buying local and organic.

All of the recipes in this book are prepared using only organic ingredients. We believe that using fresh organic ingredients is the first step in making a truly delicious meal.

Burger Basics

Hippocrates said, "Let food be thy medicine and medicine be thy food." We say, "Why not let it be in the form of a delicious veggie burger!" The benefits of a whole-foods, plant-based diet are numerous, and in this book we've taken simple, plant-based ingredients and formed them into yummy family-friendly veggie burgers.

It's important to know that veggie burgers and your traditional hamburgers, while both circular in shape, have very little in common. Veggie burgers tend to be stickier and require a bit more patience than regular ground-meat hamburgers when forming them into patties. It's helpful to keep your hands moist while forming your patty. Another option is to use a ring mold and form your patties directly on your baking sheet or skillet. Simply drop spoonfuls of the burger mixture into the mold and press down with a spoon or your fingers and then remove the mold.

All the burger recipes in this book can be both panfried or baked, and most can be grilled. When baking it's helpful to line your baking sheet with nonstick foil or parchment paper. When panfrying, it's best to use a nonstick pan. Panfrying your burgers will result in a crispier outside, while baking tends to produce a firmer burger.

When grilling your burger, there are a few key tricks to keep in mind. Vegetable and bean burgers are much lower in fat and don't have the same natural juices that a traditional meat burger has, so you need to oil your grill to prevent the burgers from sticking. Clean your grill, scraping off any bits and pieces. Then, take a paper towel dipped in oil and rub it thoroughly across the grates. Alternatively, spray your grill with a nonstick cooking spray or line it with nonstick foil. For an optimal grilling experience, it's best to use a precooked, frozen burger patty. Place your frozen patty on a preheated gas or charcoal grill and grill for approximately 5 minutes on each side or until heated through. Not all burgers are grill friendly, so we've placed handy "grill friendly" labels throughout the book to help you identify which recipes work best for grilling.

While your veggie burgers might start out a little stickier than traditional hamburgers, they will firm up once cooked. You'll find in most of our recipes we'll use either flour and/or bread crumbs. These two ingredients help to bind the burger together. While you can use store-bought bread crumbs, we like to use our own Homemade Bread Crumbs (page 108). They are slightly seasoned and are great not only in veggie burgers but added to salads, pasta, and rice. If you are gluten sensitive, make sure you use a gluten-free bread. If you do opt to purchase store-bought bread crumbs, make sure to select toasted bread crumbs, as this will more closely match the kind used in our recipes—and note the Quick Tip on the recipe page for instructions on seasoning your bread crumbs. Also, don't forget to check the ingredients label for any unnecessary fillers, additives, chemicals, or preservatives.

Storage and Reheating

All of the burgers in this book can be stored in the refrigerator or frozen if done properly. The best way to prepare the burgers for storage is to lay them in a single layer and let them cool completely. They can then be placed in an airtight container (freezer-safe if you are planning on freezing) with a layer of wax paper in between each burger. Do not stack more than two or three on top of each other. Most burgers will generally keep for about three to five days in the refrigerator and about four to six months in the freezer.

To reheat, the burgers can be microwaved but they will not be as crisp. For best results, we recommend preheating your oven to 400°F and placing the frozen patties on a nonstick or parchment-lined baking sheet. Bake for 5 to 10 minutes on each side until heated through. The burgers can also be panfried with 1 teaspoon of oil heated in a skillet over medium heat. Cook your thawed patties for 3 to 5 minutes on each side or until heated through.

Beans and Rice

You'll find that most of our recipes include either or both cooked beans and rice. Beans are a great binder for your burgers, and rice contributes good texture. You have a couple of options when it comes to using beans and rice and we'll discuss them here.

Dried beans are inexpensive and require very little effort on your part. What you will need when working with dried beans is forethought. To prepare your beans it's best to begin by rinsing them in cold water and picking out any small rocks or other debris. Place the beans in a large bowl (or a large pot) and cover with at least two inches of water. Let your beans soak for at least 6 hours (overnight or all day is even better), or until they have doubled in size. Transfer the beans to a large pot and cover with at least two inches of water. Cover with a lid and bring to a boil. Once boiling, reduce heat to medium and cook for 1 to 1½ hours until the beans are soft. Your beans are now ready to use. You can make large batches of beans and store the leftovers in freezer-safe bags in the freezer until ready to use. It's a great time saver and the extra precooked beans will come in handy for other recipes.

Canned beans will also work in our recipes and can be a great time saver if you are running late or do not have prepared dried beans on hand. If you are going to use canned beans, we highly recommend that you purchase organic beans with low or no sodium added. Also, look for cans that are labeled BPA free. BPA stands for bisphenol A. Recent studies have linked BPA to various diseases and disorders, including breast cancer, asthma, heart disease, and neurological issues.

Rice is another inexpensive ingredient that doesn't require a lot of prepping. If you have a preferred method for cooking your rice, such as a rice cooker, then you're already ahead of the game! For a simple and foolproof method, preheat your oven to 350°F. Place 1 cup of rice, 2¼ cups of water, and 1 tablespoon of oil in an 8 x 8-inch glass baking dish. Cover tightly with aluminum foil and bake for 1 hour. Remove and fluff with a fork. Use the cooked rice as is, or add it to any recipe as needed.

Stocking Your Pantry

The best way to ensure you have everything you need to prepare delicious, plant-based meals on a regular basis is to keep a well-stocked pantry. Not only will this save you loads of time by simplifying your future shopping lists, but it will make cooking with fresh, high-quality ingredients easy and joyful. Our pantry list below includes many of the items you will need to prepare the recipes in this book. If you are new to plant-based cooking, use it as a starting point for your grocery shopping list.

Nuts and Seeds:

- ❑ chia seeds
- ❑ sunflower seeds
- ❑ pumpkin seeds
- ❑ hemp seeds
- ❑ almonds
- ❑ cashews
- ❑ macadamia nuts

Beans (dried or canned):

- ❑ pinto beans
- ❑ cannellini beans
- ❑ kidney beans
- ❑ garbanzo beans
- ❑ black beans
- ❑ adzuki beans

Grains:

- ❑ quinoa
- ❑ millet
- ❑ brown rice
- ❑ lentils
- ❑ whole-wheat couscous
- ❑ old-fashioned oats

Oils:

- ❑ olive oil
- ❑ canola oil
- ❑ coconut oil
- ❑ toasted sesame oil
- ❑ sunflower oil
- ❑ safflower oil
- ❑ grapeseed oil

Flour:

- ❑ garbanzo bean flour
- ❑ millet flour
- ❑ spelt flour
- ❑ almond flour
- ❑ brown rice flour
- ❑ whole-wheat flour
- ❑ whole-wheat pastry flour

Sweeteners:

- ❑ coconut nectar
- ❑ honey
- ❑ maple syrup
- ❑ coconut crystals
- ❑ molasses

Spices and Seasoning:

- ❑ sea salt
- ❑ smoked paprika
- ❑ nutritional yeast
- ❑ oregano
- ❑ parsley

Vinegars and Sauces:

- ❑ soy sauce or tamari
- ❑ coconut aminos
- ❑ apple cider vinegar
- ❑ balsamic vinegar
- ❑ Worcestershire sauce
- ❑ brown rice or rice wine vinegar

Miscellaneous Items:

- ❑ miso (chickpea, sweet rice, or other varieties)
- ❑ low-sodium vegetable broth
- ❑ soy milk or other nondairy milk
- ❑ soy milk powder
- ❑ active dry yeast
- ❑ Dijon mustard
- ❑ Homemade Bread Crumbs (see page 108)

Frequently Asked Questions

If you are just starting out on a plant-based diet, you may have questions about some of the listed ingredients. In this section, we hope to answer your questions and provide some insight as to why we selected the ingredients we did. If you don't find the answers to all of your questions here, please feel free to contact us at info @thenakedkitchen.com and we will do our best to answer them.

You state that organic foods should be used whenever possible, but your recipes don't list the ingredients as organic. Should I buy organic products or not?

All of our recipes are made with organic ingredients. In an effort to not be overly repetitive, we don't label each ingredient as organic. While we *strongly* encourage everyone to use organic ingredients whenever possible, we understand that not everyone has access to organic items all the time.

What are coconut crystals and coconut nectar, and why are they used so often in your recipes?

Coconut crystals and coconut nectar are both plant-based sweeteners that we use in our recipes as alternatives to artificial sugars. Unlike other refined sweeteners, both coconut crystals and coconut nectar are minimally processed and still contain all their natural enzymes and nutritional value.

Why don't you use agave nectar?

Most agave "nectar" or "syrup" is nothing more than a laboratory-generated, super-condensed fructose syrup, which is devoid of virtually all nutrient value. Agave nectar has a fructose content of about 75 percent, which is much higher than that of high-fructose corn syrup, which is about 55 percent. While we try to limit the use of sweeteners in our recipes, when a sweetener is needed we prefer to use either coconut crystals or coconut nectar.

Where do you find the ingredients you use in your recipes?

We purchase most of our ingredients from our local natural grocery stores. Whole Foods also carries most of the ingredients used in our recipes. From time to time, we do purchase ingredients through online vendors, but all the ingredients featured in this book should be readily available at your local natural foods store or supermarket.

Can I switch one ingredient for another in your recipes?

Unfortunately, questions like this are nearly impossible to answer without us preparing the recipe with that exact substitution. Each recipe featured in this book was specifically created using the ingredients listed. Veggie burgers, in particular, require an exact balance of ingredients to create the right texture and flavor combination. While we encourage you to be adventurous, to experiment and play with the recipes found in this book, not all substitutions will result in a positive outcome. Whenever possible, we have indicated where substitution are acceptable.

Can I substitute my usual sweetener in place of coconut crystals or coconut nectar?

Our recipes are generally created by experimenting with ratios until we get the right formula. All of the ingredients need to work together just so to create the final product. Different sweeteners have different properties and we cannot tell you how the recipe will turn out when another sweetener is substituted for the coconut crystals or coconut nectar. Whenever possible, we have listed alternative sweeteners with which we have had good luck. While honey isn't specifically a plant-based food, we know many of our readers have easy access to honey and enjoy the health benefits that it offers, so we have listed it as a substitution whenever possible. If you follow a strict vegan diet and do not have access to coconut nectar or crystals, we encourage you to give brown rice syrup a try. It is similar in texture to honey, has a very mild taste, and is naturally gluten-free!

Many of your recipes use nutritional yeast. What is that and do I have to use it?

Nutritional yeast is a deactivated yeast as well as a source of vitamins, especially the B-complex vitamins, and a complete protein. It is also naturally low in fat and sodium and free of sugar, dairy, and gluten. Some brands of nutritional yeast, though not all, are fortified with vitamin B12. In our recipes, nutritional yeast is used for its flavor and texture. There are no substitutions for nutritional yeast and leaving it out of a recipe will drastically alter the final result and flavor, so we highly recommend having it on hand. Nutritional yeast can be purchased at most natural and health food stores. It's usually located near the protein powders and vitamins.

Many of your recipes include a neutral-flavor oil. Which oils are considered to have a neutral flavor?

Canola, grapeseed, olive, safflower, and sunflower are all neutral-flavor oils.

In many of your recipes, you use nondairy cheese and nondairy milk. If I'm a vegetarian or otherwise non-vegan, can I substitute these ingredients with cow's milk and cheeses?

In almost all cases you can easily substitute nondairy cheese for cow's milk cheese without sacrificing the end results. When a recipe calls for nondairy milk, it is generally safe to substitute with cow's milk. The only exception to this is when a recipe uses soy milk. Soy milk has certain properties that are different than other nondairy milks and cow's milk. In these cases, it is best to use soy milk to ensure a positive result.

Throughout the book I see certain recipes are labeled with one or more of the following graphics:

Why is this?

We know many of our readers follow a gluten-free diet, so for them we have identified those recipes that are gluten-free. We've done the same for our recipes that are free of soy and soy products. Any of our burgers that are labeled grill-friendly will turn out best when grilled in a precooked, frozen state. You can find specific directions under Burger Basics (page 3) for grilling all of our veggie burgers.

BEAN BURGERS

Zesty Bean Burger

This was the very first veggie burger we made for our family, and it launched our obsession with plant-based burgers. This one is full of flavor, packed with nutrients, and can be whipped up and on the table in only 30 minutes!

1¾ cups cooked garbanzo beans

1 medium carrot, finely chopped

½ medium red pepper

½ medium onion

Large handful of spinach

2 cloves garlic, minced

Dash of cayenne

2 heaping tablespoons smoked paprika

¼ cup sunflower seeds

1 tablespoon chia seeds

2 tablespoons pumpkin seeds

1 cup spelt flour (or garbanzo bean flour for a gluten-free option)

Fun Fact: This burger is extremely kid-friendly. The vegetables have all been processed, so you aren't left with any chunks or pieces and the smoked paprika gives the burger a bacon-like flavor that kids really enjoy. We recommend topping it with their favorite ketchup or some Ranch Dressing (page 125).

1. Preheat the oven to 375°F. Line a baking sheet with parchment paper or nonstick foil, and set aside.

2. Place the first 8 ingredients in a food processor and pulse until well blended. Remove the mixture and place in a large mixing bowl.

3. Add the sunflower, chia, and pumpkin seeds and mix well. Add the flour to the mixture and stir until well blended.

4. Shape the mixture into 10 patties and place them on the prepared baking sheet. Bake for 15 minutes, then flip the patties over and bake for another 10 minutes or until firm.

Makes 10 burgers.

Southwestern Mini Sliders

These burgers may be little but they are big on taste. While they are perfect for "little hands," they are loved by young and old alike. Top with a dollop of Ranch Dressing (page 125) and serve with a side of Crunchy Apple and Cabbage Salad (page 153) for a meal that everyone will love.

1¾ cups cooked black beans

Heaping ½ cup cooked brown rice

½ small red onion, finely diced

2 tablespoons diced green chilies

½ cup sweet corn (thaw if frozen)

1 clove garlic, minced

1½ teaspoons southwestern seasoning

½ teaspoon sea salt

1 tablespoon molasses

1–2 tablespoons hot sauce or to taste (optional)

½–¾ cup crushed tortilla chips of your choice

1. Preheat the oven to 350°F. Line a baking sheet with parchment paper or nonstick foil, and set aside.

2. Add the black beans to a large bowl and gently mash with a fork. Add the remaining ingredients, except the tortilla chips, and mix well.

3. In ¼ cup increments, add the tortilla chips until the mixture forms a firm ball.

4. Form into 16 to 18 small patties, about the size of a golf ball, and place on the prepared baking sheet. Bake for 10 minutes, then flip the patties over and bake for another 10 to 15 minutes or until firm.

5. Serve on dinner rolls, mini slider buns, or in a pita.

Makes 16–18 mini burgers.

Quick Tip: When purchasing tortilla chips, make sure to read the ingredients label to avoid any unnecessary additives or ingredients. Select brands that stick to the three basic ingredients—organic corn, organic oil (safflower, sunflower, canola, or olive oil) and sea salt.

Pad Thai Burger

This burger takes us back to our favorite Thai restaurant and the most delicious pad thai dish we ever had. Sadly, the restaurant no longer exists, but the flavor of its pad thai lives on in this recipe. If you like a spicy pad thai, feel free to add a little hot sauce to the mix.

½ cup chopped carrots

½ cup chopped diakon radish

1¾ cups cooked garbanzo beans

2 green onions, diced

2 tablespoons roughly chopped fresh cilantro

3 tablespoons creamy peanut butter

1 tablespoon freshly squeezed lime juice

2 tablespoons toasted sesame oil

2 cloves garlic, minced

2 teaspoons minced ginger

2 tablespoons soy sauce or tamari (gluten-free if needed)

½ cup millet flour

1. Preheat the oven to 350°F. Line a baking sheet with parchment paper or nonstick foil, and set aside.

2. Place all the ingredients, except the flour, in a food processor and pulse only until just well blended. Do not over-process.

3. Transfer the mixture to a mixing bowl, add in the flour, and mix well.

4. Shape the mixture into 6 patties and place on the prepared baking sheet. Bake for 30 minutes, then flip the patties over and bake for another 20 minutes or until firm.

Makes 6 burgers.

Quick Tip: When it comes to peanut butter, not all brands are created equal. When shopping for peanut butter, look for brands with only one ingredient—organic peanuts! Skip the brands that have added sugars and salt.

Pizza Burger

Deep dish or thin crust? Mushrooms or pineapple? Now you don't have to decide. Everyone will love this pizza-inspired burger. Pick from an assortment of your favorite toppings and enjoy!

1. Preheat the oven to 425°F. Line a baking sheet with parchment paper or nonstick foil, and set aside.

2. In a large bowl, use a fork to gently mash the beans. Add the remaining ingredients and mix until well blended.

3. Shape the mixture into 8 patties and place on the prepared baking sheet. Bake for 20 minutes, then flip the patties over and bake for another 15 to 20 minutes or until firm.

Makes 8 burgers.

1¾ cups cooked cannellini beans

1½ cups cooked barley

½ cup tomato paste

½ cup Homemade Bread Crumbs (page 108)

¼ cup diced red onion

3–4 cloves garlic, minced

1 teaspoon oregano

¼ cup nutritional yeast

¼ cup whole-grain flour (whole wheat, spelt, or millet)

Fun Fact: Barley is an ancient grain that is sadly overlooked by today's culinary world, yet it is one of the grains with the greatest health benefits, flavor, and versatility. It helps to lower blood cholesterol levels, aids digestion, and, because it's a good source of selenium, it has been shown to significantly reduce the risk of colon cancer. Barley can be used as a delicious breakfast cereal, in soups and stews, and as a rice substitute for dishes such as risotto.

Greek "Chicken" Burger

This burger is a bit of a cross between a chicken tender and a falafel. It's really delicious served in a pita with tomatoes, onions, cucumbers, and our Ranch Dressing (page 125).

1. Process the garbanzo beans in a food processor until coarsely ground but not mushy. You can also mash them with a fork if you prefer. Transfer to a mixing bowl.

2. Add the carrot to the food processor and pulse a few times, then add the zucchini and process until coarsely ground, or shred the carrot and zucchini with a hand grater. Add to the bowl with the beans.

3. Add the remaining ingredients except the flour and oil and mix to combine. Then fold in the flour until completely mixed. The mixture should be sticky but hold together.

4. Form the burger mixture into 8 patties. Heat 1 tablespoon of the oil in a large nonstick skillet over medium-high heat. Place the patties in the skillet and brown for 3 to 4 minutes on each side, adding more oil if necessary when flipping. You may have to work in batches, depending on the size of your skillet.

5. Reduce the heat to low and let the burgers cook for an additional 10 to 15 minutes on each side until firm.

Makes 8 patties.

Fun Fact: Garbanzo beans, also known as chickpeas, are consumed more than any other legume in the world. The nutty-flavored beans originated in the Middle East and are grown mainly in India. Just ½ cup of garbanzo beans provides you with 6 grams of protein and 5 grams of fiber. They are also rich in magnesium, potassium, and iron.

1¾ cups cooked garbanzo beans

1 medium carrot, roughly chopped

1 small zucchini, roughly chopped

3 tablespoons Chickenless Bouillon Mix (recipe on next page)

2 tablespoons soft silken tofu

Juice of 1 lemon or about 2 tablespoons

1 teaspoon coconut aminos, soy sauce, or tamari (gluten-free if needed)

½ teaspoon cumin

½ teaspoon sea salt

⅛ teaspoon ground white pepper

½ cup garbanzo bean flour

1–2 tablespoons olive oil or other neutral-flavor oil

Chickenless Bouillon Mix

If you look at the ingredients list on a box of bouillon cubes, you may have a hard time even pronouncing most of the ingredients. In this mix we've eliminated all those unhealthy ingredients without sacrificing any of the flavor.

¼ cup nutritional yeast

2 teaspoons onion powder

½ teaspoon garlic powder

¼ teaspoon sea salt

½ teaspoon thyme

½ teaspoon parsley

⅛ teaspoon ground sage leaf
   (aka rubbed sage)

⅛ teaspoon rosemary,
   crushed or ground

Pinch of turmeric

Pinch of celery seed

Place all the ingredients in a small bowl and mix well. Store in a cool, dry place for up to 1 year.

Makes approximately ⅓ cup.

Quick Tip: Preheat your oven to 450°F. Dice a few of your favorite potatoes and place them on a nonstick baking sheet. Drizzle with olive oil and sprinkle with Chickenless Bouillon Mix. Place the potatoes in the oven and let them cook for about 30 to 35 minutes or until tender and golden brown, turning over halfway through cooking. These flavorful roasted potatoes make an ideal side dish for many of our burgers.

Cheesy Burrito Burger

If you love a good burrito, you'll want to give this recipe a try. Skip the traditional ketchup and top your burger with guacamole, lettuce, and onions instead. *Yum!*

1. Preheat the oven to 375°F. Line a baking sheet with parchment paper or nonstick foil, and set aside.

2. Mix together all the ingredients in a large bowl. Form into 8 patties and place on the prepared baking sheet. Bake for 15 minutes, then flip the patties over and bake for another 20 minutes or until firm.

Makes 8 burgers.

- 1¾ **cups low-fat refried beans**
- 1½ **cups cooked brown rice**
- 4 **ounces finely diced green chilies**
- ¾ **cup of your favorite enchilada sauce (homemade or store-bought)**
- ½ **cup vital wheat gluten**
- ¾ **cup Homemade Bread Crumbs (page 108)**
- ½ **cup nutritional yeast**

Quick Tip: While we love making homemade refried beans, sometimes we run short on time and need to open a can instead. Our favorite brand of refried beans is Amy's Vegetarian Organic Refried Beans (they are vegan friendly, too!). If you can't find Amy's brand in your local store, look for a product that contains just a few simple ingredients, such as organic beans, onion, organic oil (usually canola, sunflower or safflower), salt, garlic, and spices.

BBQ Chickpea Burger

Sometimes life just calls for a good dose of barbecued goodness. Add a dab of sauce and top with some creamy coleslaw for the perfect BBQ burger.

1. Preheat the oven to 400°F. Line a baking sheet with parchment paper or nonstick foil, and set aside.

2. Place the first four ingredients in a food processor and pulse until just slightly blended. Remove the mixture and place in a large mixing bowl.

3. Add the barbecue sauce, smoked paprika, sea salt, bread crumbs, and vinegar and mix well. Add the flour to the mixture and stir well until blended.

4. Shape the mixture into 10 patties and place on the prepared baking sheet. Bake for 20 minutes, then flip the patties over and bake for another 10 to 20 minutes or until firm.

Makes 10 burgers.

- 1¾ cups cooked garbanzo beans
- ½ cup chopped red onion
- ½ cup broccoli florets
- 1 medium carrot, chopped
- ¼ cup plus 3 tablespoons Sweet and Tangy BBQ Sauce (page 119) or any barbecue sauce of your choice
- 1½ teaspoons smoked paprika
- ½ teaspoon sea salt
- 1 cup Homemade Bread Crumbs (page 108)
- 2 tablespoons apple cider vinegar
- 6 tablespoons garbanzo bean flour

Quick Tip: Smoked paprika is a Spanish cousin to the more widely used sweet Hungarian paprika. It's made from pimiento peppers that have been dried and smoked over an oak fire, then ground into a fine powder. Not all smoked paprika is created equal. Flavors and smokiness vary greatly between brands. Our favorite brand is McCormick Smoked Paprika, which is what we used to create the recipes in this book.

Miso Ginger Mung Bean Burger

Mung beans are delicious beans that just don't get the recognition they deserve. In this recipe they pair perfectly with the pickled ginger, and the miso adds a depth of flavor to the whole dish. Enjoy this burger as is, or add it to your favorite stir-fry or veggie salad.

1½ cups cooked mung beans

1 cup cooked quinoa

¼ cup Miso Madness Dressing (recipe on next page)

3 tablespoons finely chopped pickled ginger

½ teaspoon sea salt

1 tablespoon potato starch

½ cup unseasoned toasted bread crumbs (gluten-free if needed)

1 tablespoon apple cider vinegar

2 cloves garlic, minced

½ tablespoon cumin

½ teaspoon smoked paprika

½ teaspoon chili powder

1 tablespoon freshly squeezed lime juice

1. Preheat the oven to 425°F. Line a baking sheet with parchment paper or nonstick foil, and set aside.

2. Add the mung beans to a large bowl and gently mash with a fork. Add the remaining ingredients to the bowl and mix well.

3. Form the mixture into 5 patties and place on the prepared baking sheet. Bake for 25 minutes, then flip the patties over and bake for another 20 minutes or until firm.

Makes 5 burgers.

Miso Madness Dressing

This creamy dressing has just the right hint of tang that makes it ideal for dressing up salads, pasta, vegetables, and rice dishes.

Place all of the ingredients, except the oil, in a blender or food processor. Pulse a few times and then slowly pour in the oil while the mixture blends on high speed. After all the oil is added, you should have a smooth, creamy consistency.

This dressing can be stored in an airtight container in the refrigerator for up to 2 weeks.

Makes 3 cups.

½ cup miso of your choice (chickpea or sweet miso work great)

½ cup apple cider vinegar

¼ cup plus 3 tablespoons reduced-sodium soy sauce or tamari (gluten-free if needed)

½ medium sweet or yellow onion

1 tablespoon coconut nectar, honey, or brown rice syrup (optional)

¾ cup safflower oil or other neutral-flavor oil (not olive oil)

Fun Fact: Made from fermented soybeans, miso is a thick paste–like substance. Miso is usually yellow or brownish in color and tastes salty and tangy on its own. Besides soy, miso can also be made from barley, rice, chickpeas, or other grains. These types of miso will vary in color and taste, though most can be used interchangeably in recipes.

Asian Quinoa Burger

This burger is inspired by one of our favorite recipes, Quinoa Lettuce Wraps (which you can find at www.thenakedkitchen.com). It has just the right amount of crunch and a savory flavor that will bring you back for seconds. You can serve this burger on a traditional bun, but it also pairs beautifully with rice or crumbled up and tossed with your favorite salad.

1¾ cups cooked black beans

1 large carrot, finely diced

8 ounces whole water chestnuts, finely diced

1½ cups cooked quinoa

2 green onions, finely diced

3–4 cloves garlic, minced

¼ cup reduced-sodium soy sauce, tamari or coconut aminos (gluten-free if needed)

2 tablespoons toasted sesame oil

2 teaspoons minced ginger

1 tablespoon coconut nectar, honey, or brown rice syrup

2 tablespoons brown rice vinegar

1 cup brown rice flour

1. Preheat the oven to 400°F. Line a baking sheet with parchment paper or nonstick foil, and set aside.

2. In a large bowl, add the black beans and gently mash them with a fork. Stir in the remaining ingredients, except the flour, and mix well. Finally, add the flour and mix until incorporated.

3. Shape the mixture into 10 patties and place on the prepared baking sheet. Bake for 20 to 25 minutes, then flip the patties over and bake for another 20 minutes or until firm.

Makes 10 burgers.

Fun Fact: Did you know that quinoa, although referred to as a grain, is actually a seed from a vegetable related to Swiss chard, spinach, and beets? Quinoa (pronounced keen–wa) is considered one of the most important "superfoods" in the world. It is a complete protein, containing all 9 essential amino acids, has almost twice as much fiber as other grains, and is rich in iron (which increases brain function) and magnesium (which reduces Type 2 diabetes by promoting healthy blood sugar control). When cooking quinoa, try replacing the water with a flavorful vegetable broth for a better-tasting result.

Adzuki Bean Burger

This recipe takes seven simple ingredients and turns them into a crispy and delicious burger that is perfect on a bun, in a pita, or crumbled up and added to your favorite salad. (Note: If you can't find adzuki beans at your local grocery store, you can substitute kidney beans or any other red bean.)

1. Preheat the oven to 400°F. Line a baking sheet with parchment paper or nonstick foil, and set aside.

2. In a large bowl, use a fork to mash the beans. Add in the remaining ingredients and mix until well blended.

3. Shape into 8 patties and place on the prepared baking sheet. Bake for 40 minutes, then flip the patties over and bake for another 15 minutes or until firm.

Makes 8 burgers.

1¾ cups cooked adzuki beans
1 cup cooked quinoa
1½ cups cooked millet
½ cup mashed sweet potato
½ cup coconut oil, not melted
¼ cup chopped green chilies
¼ cup diced red onion

Fun Fact: Millet is a grain that should be in everyone's pantry! Along with being gluten-free and non-allergenic, it's also alkaline and extremely easy to digest. The serotonin in millet can calm your moods and the magnesium can help to reduce the effects of migraines and the likelihood of heart attacks. Millet is high in protein and rich in vitamins and antioxidants, making it an ideal grain to incorporate in your diet.

Spicy Chili Burger

When we first made this burger, we ate it so quickly that it didn't even make it onto a bun! It has since become one of our favorite burgers. This recipe is very versatile, so we often make a double batch to freeze and have on hand for Beyond Burger recipes. For classic results, we prefer to panfry them, but for a healthier version, bake them per the instructions at the end of this recipe.

1¾ cups cooked kidney beans

1½ cups cooked brown rice

½ cup shelled hemp seeds

¼ cup diced red onion

½ cup finely chopped kale

3 cloves garlic, minced

⅓ cup corn (thaw if frozen)

3 tablespoons Sweet Heat
   Chili Sauce (page 111)

¼ cup plus 2 tablespoons
   nutritional yeast

1 tablespoon apple cider
   vinegar

½ teaspoon sea salt

1 teaspoon ancho chili
   powder

¼ teaspoon cayenne or to
   taste

½–1 cup spelt flour

1–2 tablespoons olive oil or
   other neutral-flavor oil

1. Place the kidney beans in a large mixing bowl and gently mash them with a fork.

2. Toss in the remaining ingredients, except the flour and olive oil, and stir until well incorporated.

3. Add the flour in ¼-cup increments just until the mixture holds together (you might not need all the flour). Shape the mixture into 6 to 8 patties.

4. Heat 1 tablespoon of the oil in a large sauté pan. Once the pan is preheated, cook the patties for about 3 to 4 minutes on each side or until heated through and lightly crisped, adding more oil if necessary.

No-Fry Method: For step 4, preheat the oven to 375°F. Place the patties on a parchment- or foil-lined baking sheet and bake for 20 to 30 minutes or until firm, flipping them over halfway through.

Makes 6–8 burgers.

Fun Fact: If you've never worked with hemp seeds before, now is the time to start! Hemp is a high-protein seed containing all twenty amino acids, including the nine essential amino acids (EAAs) our bodies cannot produce. It also has high amounts of fatty acids and fiber as well as vitamin E and trace minerals. Hemp has a balanced 3:1 ratio of omega-3 to omega-6 fats and is one of the most easily digested vegetarian and vegan protein sources.

Buffalo Black Bean Burger

After one of our taste testers asked us to create a burger featuring his favorite type of sauce—buffalo sauce—this is the burger we came up with. The simple flavors really let the buffalo flavor shine through. Here's our buffalo sauce-inspired burger in all its delicious glory!

1. Preheat the oven to 400°F. Line a baking sheet with parchment paper or nonstick foil, and set aside.

2. Place the black beans in a large bowl and, using a fork, mash about 50 percent of the beans, leaving the other 50 percent whole.

3. Add the onion, garlic, corn, soy sauce, mashed potatoes, and seasoning to the black beans and mix well. Add in ¼ cup of bread crumbs at a time until the burger mixture starts to hold together.

4. Form the mixture into 6 patties and place on the prepared baking sheet. Bake for 25 minutes, then flip the burgers over and continue baking for an additional 20 minutes or until the burgers are cooked through. (Alternatively, you can panfry the burgers in a large skillet. Heat the oil on medium-high heat and cook for about 3 to 4 minutes on each side or until firm and slightly crispy.)

Makes 6 burgers.

- 1¾ cups cooked black beans
- ½ cup diced yellow onion
- 2 cloves garlic, minced
- ½ cup corn (thaw if frozen)
- 2 tablespoons reduced-sodium soy sauce or tamari (gluten-free if needed)
- 1 cup cooked mashed potatoes
- 3 tablespoons Buffalo Sauce Seasoning (recipe on next page)
- ½–¾ cup Homemade Bread Crumbs (page 108)
- 1 teaspoon olive oil or other neutral-flavor oil (if panfrying)

Fun Fact: A cup of black beans packs a whopping 15 grams of satisfying protein and doesn't contain any of the saturated fat found in other protein sources, such as red meat. Considering that black beans contain at least eight different flavonoids with enormous antioxidant potential, and their high content of phytochemicals, it's hardly surprising that studies have connected black bean consumption with reduced risk of certain cancers. Recent studies have suggested considerable effectiveness against colon adenoma, a non-cancerous tumor that can progress into colon cancer.

Buffalo Sauce Seasoning

If you're a fan of traditional buffalo sauce, you'll want to give this seasoning a try. It's fantastic for sprinkling on baked potatoes, popcorn, or your favorite french fries.

¼ cup coconut crystals or other dry sweetener of your choice

½ tablespoon chili powder

½ tablespoon smoked paprika

½ teaspoon cumin

¼–½ teaspoon cayenne

1 tablespoon garlic powder

½ tablespoon mustard powder

½ tablespoon sea salt

¼ tablespoon black pepper

Place all the ingredients in a small blender and pulse 2 to 3 times. Store in an airtight container in a cool, dark place for up to 6 months.

Makes approximately ½ cup.

Quick Tip: Sweet and flavorful carrots pair perfectly with this Buffalo Sauce Seasoning and make an ideal side dish to any of our burgers. Cut 3 or 4 carrots in ¼-inch pieces and add to a mixing bowl. Drizzle with 2 to 3 tablespoons of olive oil and add in 1 to 2 tablespoons of seasoning. Stir until well coated. Spread the carrots in an even layer on a nonstick baking sheet and place in a preheated oven at 350°F for 15 to 20 minutes or until the carrots are tender and slightly browned. Serve immediately.

Thin and Crispy "Chicken Sandwich" Burger

You'll love this healthy and sustainable chickenless burger. Top it off with some creamy Dijonnaise, crisp lettuce, and juicy tomato slices for the perfect lunch or dinner.

1. Use a fork or potato masher to mash the garbanzo beans until no whole beans are left. Transfer to a large mixing bowl.

2. Add the remaining ingredients and, using your hands, knead together for about 5 minutes or until strings start to form when pulled apart.

3. Form the dough into 14 to 16 thin patties about 2 to 3 inches wide.

4. Heat a tablespoon of oil in a large sauté pan over medium-high heat. Working in batches if necessary, cook the patties for about 2 to 3 minutes per side or until golden brown.

5. Remove the cooked patties and place on a plate to rest for about 5 minutes before serving.

Makes 14–16 burgers.

1¾ cups cooked garbanzo
   beans
¼ cup olive oil, plus 1 to 2
   tablespoons for frying
1 cup vital wheat gluten
1 cup Homemade Bread
   Crumbs (page 108)
½ cup vegetable broth
½ cup soy sauce or tamari
1 clove garlic, minced
2 tablespoons Chickenless
   Bouillon Mix (page 20)

Quick Tip: For a kid-friendly "nugget," take 1 tablespoon of dough and gently flatten between your palms. Continue cooking as instructed and serve with ketchup or Ranch Dressing (page 125).

Caribbean Spinach Burger

Take a little trip to the tropics. Coconut and ginger flavor this spinach burger with a taste of the Caribbean.

1 tablespoon olive oil or other neutral-flavor oil

½ medium onion, diced

1 teaspoon salt, divided

5 ounces fresh baby spinach, chopped (about 2½ cups)

2 cloves garlic, minced

1-inch piece of ginger, peeled and minced

1 teaspoon red pepper flakes or to taste

1¾ cups cooked garbanzo beans

½ cup unseasoned toasted bread crumbs (gluten-free if needed)

⅓ cup nutritional yeast

¼ cup shredded coconut

¼ cup coconut milk

Juice of half a lime (use other half for the Pineapple Relish)

Pineapple Relish, optional garnish (page 113)

1. Preheat the oven to 350°F. Line a baking sheet with parchment paper, and set aside.

2. Heat a skillet over medium-high heat and add the oil. Add the onions and ½ teaspoon of the salt. Cook until the onions are tender, about 5 minutes.

3. Add the spinach, garlic, ginger, red pepper flakes, and remaining salt. Cook until the spinach has wilted, about 2 to 3 minutes.

4. Place the garbanzo beans in a food processor and pulse a few times to chop. Add the onion-and-spinach mixture and pulse several times until finely chopped.

5. Add the bread crumbs, nutritional yeast, shredded coconut, coconut milk, and lime juice. Pulse until mixed.

6. Form the mixture into 8 patties. Place the patties on the prepared baking sheet and bake for 10 minutes, then turn them over and bake for 10 minutes more or until lightly browned.

7. Serve immediately and garnish with Pineapple Relish if desired.

Makes 8 burgers.

Fun Fact: Did you know that cooking spinach actually increases its health benefits! Just half a cup of cooked spinach will give you three times as much nutrition as one cup of raw spinach. That's because the body cannot completely break down the nutrients in raw spinach for optimal absorption.

Mushroom and Lentil Burger

This burger is rich and meaty, but its real beauty is its versatility. You can top this burger with just about anything and have a whole new meal each time.

1. Heat a large skillet over medium-high heat and add 1 tablespoon of the oil.

2. Add the onions and ½ teaspoon salt, cook 3 to 4 minutes or until the onions start to soften.

3. Add 1 tablespoon more of the oil, then add the mushrooms, garlic, thyme, pepper, and the remaining ½ teaspoon of salt. Cook until the vegetables are tender, about 5 to 6 minutes.

4. Pour in the coconut aminos and cook until the liquid has been absorbed. Transfer the vegetables to the bowl of a food processor. Add the remaining ingredients and pulse until combined.

5. Form the mixture into 8 patties. Wipe out the skillet used to cook the vegetables and heat over medium-high heat. Add ½ tablespoon of the oil and cook 4 of the patties for about 5 minutes on each side or until nicely browned and firm. Repeat with the remaining ½ tablespoon of oil and patties.

Makes 8 burgers.

Fun Fact: Lentils are a true nutritional powerhouse, as they are loaded with fiber, folate, iron, protein, and other vitamins and minerals. Lentils help to lower cholesterol, reduce the risk of heart disease, prevent constipation, increase energy, aid in weight loss, and stabilize blood sugar.

3 tablespoons olive oil, divided

1 medium onion, roughly chopped (about 1 cup)

1 teaspoon sea salt, divided

8 ounces cremini mushrooms, roughly chopped (about 2 cups)

2 cloves garlic, minced

1 teaspoon thyme

½ teaspoon black pepper

2 tablespoons coconut aminos, soy sauce, or tamari (gluten-free if needed)

1 cup cooked lentils (French green or brown work well, but don't overcook)

½ cup unseasoned toasted bread crumbs (gluten-free if needed)

¼ cup Cashew Parmesan (see page 132)

2 tablespoons soy milk powder

2 tablespoons Dijon mustard

2 tablespoons minced fresh parsley

1 teaspoon lemon zest

Bistro Burger

This burger is inspired by that "just off the grill" flavor you get at a bistro. Serve it with grilled corn and a cold drink for the full effect.

Heaping ½ cup coarsely chopped cremini mushrooms

1 cup cooked brown rice

¼ cup diced red onion

Heaping ¼ cup coarsely chopped carrot

¼ cup diced red bell pepper

2 cloves garlic, minced

½ cup cooked shelled soy beans (edamame)

1¾ cups cooked pinto beans

1 tablespoon olive oil

1 teaspoon sea salt

2 tablespoons soy sauce or tamari (gluten-free if needed)

2 tablespoons apple cider vinegar

1 tablespoon molasses

½ teaspoon mustard powder

A dash or two of liquid smoke

Black pepper to taste

1 cup garbanzo bean flour

1. Preheat the oven to 400°F. Line a baking sheet with parchment paper or nonstick foil and set aside.

2. Place the first 7 ingredients in a food processor and pulse until finely chopped. Do not overprocess.

3. Add the pinto beans and pulse 2 or 3 times or until the beans are broken apart.

4. Remove the mixture and place in a large mixing bowl. Add the oil, sea salt, soy sauce, vinegar, molasses, mustard powder, liquid smoke, and black pepper. Mix well.

5. Add the flour to the mixture in ¼-cup increments and stir well until blended.

6. Shape the mixture into 8 to 10 patties and place on the prepared baking sheet. Place in the oven and bake for 15 minutes, then flip the patties over and bake for another 10 to 15 minutes or until firm.

Makes 8–10 burgers.

Italian Lentil Sliders

We first made these for a holiday party we were hosting and they quickly became a family favorite. These sliders are a perfect size for children's little hands. They can also be served with pasta, on a sub sandwich, or even on their own with Ranch Dressing (page 125).

½ cup cooked brown lentils

1 cup cooked brown rice

¼ cup old-fashioned oats

¼ cup vital wheat gluten

½ cup tomato paste

⅛ cup Homemade Bread
   Crumbs (page 108)

2 tablespoons soy sauce or
   tamari

2 tablespoons olive oil or
   other neutral-flavor oil

2 teaspoons freshly squeezed
   lemon juice

¼ cup whole-wheat flour

1 teaspoon balsamic vinegar

½ teaspoon chili powder

½ teaspoon garlic powder

1 teaspoon onion powder

2 teaspoons mustard powder

2 teaspoons molasses

Sea salt to taste

18–20 slider buns of your
   choice

1 cup of your favorite
   marinara sauce

Nondairy shredded
   mozzarella cheese of your
   choice (optional garnish)

1. Preheat the oven to 350°F. Line a baking sheet with parchment paper or nonstick foil, and set aside.

2. In a large bowl, mix all the ingredients together until well combined. Scooping out approximately 3 tablespoons of the mixture at a time, use your hands to form it into balls.

3. Place the lentil balls on the prepared baking sheet and gently press down on the tops.

4. Bake for 20 minutes, then flip the sliders over and bake for an additional 15 minutes or until firm.

5. Remove the sliders from the oven and let stand for 5 minutes. Serve on your favorite mini-burger bun or roll and top with marinara sauce and shredded cheese (if using).

Makes 18–20 sliders.

Fun Fact: Prior to 1985 there were four scientifically recognized basic tastes: sweet, sour, bitter, and salty. In 1985 a fifth taste was added—umami. Umami is considered to be a savory taste, and one that greatly enhances many dishes. Soy sauce (or tamari) is ideal for adding umami to recipes. Along with soy sauce, foods such as tomatoes, soybeans, sweet potatoes, carrots, kombu, and shiitake mushrooms are rich in umami flavor.

Dukkah Spiced Burger

Dukkah is a nut-seed-and-spice mixture that originates from the Middle East. It can be used in a variety of ways, a favorite being to dip bread or vegetables into oil and then into the dukkah. This burger gets its fabulous flavor from the *dukkah*.

⅓ cup raw pistachios

2 tablespoons sesame seeds

2 tablespoons coriander seeds

1 tablespoon cumin seeds

1 tablespoon lemon thyme (3–4 fresh stems), finely minced

1 teaspoon sea salt, divided

2 tablespoons olive oil, divided

½ red onion, diced

6 ounces cremini or white button mushrooms, diced

2 cloves garlic, minced

¼ teaspoon ground black pepper

¼ cup white wine

5 ounces (about 2 cups packed) baby spinach

2–3 pitas processed into bread crumbs (gluten-free if needed)

1 cup cooked garbanzo beans, finely chopped

1. Toast the pistachios in a dry skillet over medium heat, stirring occasionally, until fragrant, 3 to 4 minutes. Place them on a cutting board and finely chop. Place in a bowl.

2. In the same skillet, toast the sesame seeds over medium heat, stirring occasionally, until a light golden color, 2 to 3 minutes. Add to the bowl with the pistachios.

3. Toast the coriander and cumin seeds in the same skillet over medium heat, stirring occasionally, until fragrant, 2 to 3 minutes. Place in a spice mill to cool. Once cooled, process until finely ground and add to the bowl of pistachios and sesame seeds.

4. Add the lemon thyme and ½ teaspoon of the sea salt and set the dukkah spice mixture aside.

5. Preheat the oven to 350°F. Line a baking sheet with parchment paper, and set aside.

6. Heat a skillet over medium-high heat. Add 1 tablespoon of the oil, the onions, and the remaining salt. Sauté for 2 to 3 minutes until softened.

7. Add the remaining 1 tablespoon of oil, mushrooms, garlic, and pepper. Cook 4 to 5 minutes or until the vegetables are tender.

8. Carefully add the wine and spinach and cook until the liquid is absorbed and the spinach has wilted.

9. Add the mushroom-and-spinach mixture, half of the pita crumbs, garbanzo beans, and all of the dukkah spice to a food processor. Pulse one or twice until just mixed. Add more crumbs until the mixture holds together when pressed in your hand.

10. Form the mixture into 8 patties and place on the prepared baking sheet. Bake for 10 minutes, then flip and bake another 6 to 8 minutes or until lightly browned and firm.

Makes 8 burgers.

Quick Tip: Lemon thyme looks just like regular thyme, but when you crush a few of its leaves and breathe in its sweet, lemony aroma, you'll be able to tell the difference. It delivers a soft herbal thyme flavor along with a subtle essence of lemon, all without any of the bitterness you sometimes get from regular thyme.

Pecan-Crusted Sweet Potato Burger

This burger is also known as a BLD—because it's great for breakfast, lunch, or dinner. Serve it between slices of toasted nut or cinnamon bread and topped with a spoonful of yogurt for a slightly sweet breakfast meal. For a more savory lunch or dinner burger, top with our versatile Avocado Relish (page 130). The bright citrus of the relish and the kick of the chili pepper balance the sweet maple-cinnamon flavor of the burger.

1. Place the pecans and ½ teaspoon of the salt in the bowl of a food processor and process until finely ground. Remove to a plate or pie pan and set aside.

2. Place the sweet potatoes, beans, parsley, soy sauce, maple syrup, ancho chili powder, cinnamon, chipotle powder, black pepper, and remaining ½ teaspoon salt in the food processor. Pulse a couple of times until mixed.

3. Add ¾ cup of the flour and process until combined. The mixture will be a little sticky but should be firm enough to shape into balls. Add the remaining flour if it's too sticky to work with. Shape into 8 to 10 thin patties. Keep your hands moistened with water to make shaping the patties easier.

4. Place each patty in the ground pecans, pressing down gently. Flip and do the same on the other side.

5. Heat 2 tablespoons of oil in a nonstick skillet over medium-high heat. Add 4 patties to the pan and cook for 4 to 5 minutes on each side until browned. Reduce heat to low and cook another 5 minutes on each side until firm. Repeat with the remaining oil and patties.

Makes 8–10 patties.

¾ **cup pecans**

1 **teaspoon sea salt, divided**

2 **sweet potatoes, baked and peeled**

2 **cups cooked cannellini beans**

2 **tablespoons minced fresh parsley**

1 **tablespoon soy sauce or tamari**

1 **tablespoon maple syrup**

1 **teaspoon ancho chili powder**

½ **teaspoon cinnamon**

¼ **teaspoon chipotle powder**

⅛ **teaspoon black pepper**

¾–1 **cup whole-wheat flour**

4 **tablespoons canola oil or other neutral-flavor oil**

Fun Fact: Does your maple syrup make the grade? In the United States maple syrup is divided into grades A and B. Grade A maple syrup typically has a milder flavor, is light in color, and is best used as a table syrup. Grade B maple syrup is darker in color, higher in nutritional value, and has a rich, maple flavor. Grade B syrups are best for cooking and baking.

VEGETABLE BURGERS

Zucchini Almond Burger

If you're new to the world of veggie burgers, this is a great introduction. The roasted almonds add amazing flavor and provide a hearty texture. This burger is sure to become a family favorite.

2-3 tablespoons olive oil or other neutral-flavor oil for frying, divided

1 cup finely diced onion

1 clove garlic, minced

1½ cups shredded zucchini (skin left on)

1 cup roasted almonds

1¾ cups cooked garbanzo beans

2 tablespoons Dijon mustard

1 tablespoon freshly squeezed lemon juice

1 teaspoon smoked paprika

1 tablespoon roughly chopped fresh oregano

2 tablespoons roughly chopped fresh parsley

1 teaspoon sea salt

1 cup cooked whole-wheat couscous

½ cup garbanzo bean flour

1. Heat 1 tablespoon of the oil in a sauté pan over medium-high heat. Sauté the onion and garlic until tender. Add the zucchini and continue to sauté until the zucchini is cooked through, about 3 to 4 minutes. Transfer to a large mixing bowl and set aside.

2. Process the almonds in a food processor to a sand-like consistency. Add the garbanzo beans, mustard, lemon juice, paprika, oregano, parsley, salt, and couscous to the food processor and pulse 4 or 5 times until the garbanzo beans are broken down. Remove the mixture and place in the mixing bowl with the zucchini and onions.

3. Using your hands or a spatula, stir the burger mixture well. Add in the garbanzo bean flour and mix once more until everything is thoroughly incorporated. Shape the mixture into 8 to 10 burger patties.

4. Heat 1 tablespoon of oil in a sauté pan on medium heat. Working in batches and adding more oil as needed, cook the patties for about 5 minutes on each side or until they are a golden brown.

Makes 8–10 burgers.

Fun Fact: Did you know that almonds have more fiber, protein, and other nutrients than any other nuts? Almonds help to reduce the risk of a heart attack, lower bad cholesterol, build strong bones and teeth, provide healthy fats, aid weight loss, lower the rise of blood sugar after meals, and nourish the nervous system.

Beet That Burger

Even if you don't love beets, we bet you'll find them sweet and delicious when mixed with roasted vegetables in this burger.

1. Combine the rice, lentils, and broth in a stock pot and bring to a boil. Reduce heat to low, cover, and simmer until the liquid is gone and the rice is tender, approximately 50 minutes. Stir and set aside to cool.

2. In a large nonstick skillet, heat 2 tablespoons of the oil over medium-high heat. Add the remaining ingredients and sauté until tender, about 8 to 10 minutes.

3. Add the vegetables to the lentil-and-rice mixture. Stir to combine, and form the mixture into 12 patties.

4. Wipe out the skillet with a damp towel. Heat the remaining teaspoon of oil in the skillet over medium heat and add the patties. You may have to cook them in batches.

5. Cook approximately 10 to 12 minutes on each side or until lightly browned.

Makes 12 burgers.

- 1 cup brown rice, uncooked
- 1 cup dried lentils (French green or crimson work best), uncooked
- 4 cups low-sodium vegetable broth
- 2 tablespoons plus 1 teaspoon olive oil, divided
- 2 large carrots, shredded
- 1 medium onion, diced
- 1 large beet, shredded
- 2 tablespoons minced fresh parsley
- 1 teaspoon rosemary
- 1 teaspoon thyme
- 1 teaspoon sea salt
- ½ teaspoon ground white pepper

Fun Fact: *Forget what you've heard about oysters; beets are a true aphrodisiac! Beets contain high amounts of boron, which is directly related to the production of human sex hormones. Beets also contain betaine, the same substance that is used in certain treatments for depression, along with tryptophan, which relaxes the mind and creates a sense of well-being.*

Pumpkin Hemp Seed Burger

This beautiful burger has all the colors of fall in its ingredients, but don't let that stop you from making it year-round.

2 tablespoons olive oil, divided

3 large shallots, finely diced

1 medium red pepper, finely diced

2 cloves garlic, minced

½ cup fresh or frozen corn

2 tablespoons Sweet Heat Chili Sauce (page 111)

1 teaspoon cumin

8 ounces pumpkin puree

½ cup shelled hemp seeds, ground

½ cup nutritional yeast

½ cup unseasoned toasted bread crumbs (finely ground and gluten-free if needed)

2 tablespoons minced parsley

Sea salt to taste

1. Heat 1 tablespoon of the oil in a large nonstick skillet over medium heat. Add the shallots and red pepper and cook until soft, about 5 minutes. Add the garlic and cook 1 to 2 minutes more.

2. Stir in the corn, chili sauce, and cumin. Cook 2 to 3 minutes more until all the flavors have blended together.

3. Transfer to a bowl and add the pumpkin, hemp seeds, nutritional yeast, bread crumbs, parsley, and salt. Stir until combined.

4. Wipe out the skillet with a damp paper towel and dry, then heat the remaining tablespoon of olive oil over medium heat.

5. Form the burger mixture into 6 patties and place in the skillet. Cook 4 to 5 minutes on each side until browned and heated through. Lower the heat and let cook an additional few minutes on each side for a nice, crispy texture.

Makes 6 burgers.

Fun Fact: Did you know that pumpkin is an excellent source of many antioxidant vitamins such as vitamins A, C, and E? It is also a rich source of minerals, including copper, calcium, potassium, and phosphorus; and, because it is high in beta-carotene, it helps to decrease your risk of many types of cancer.

Hearty Mushroom Burger

This hearty burger boasts crispy potatoes, oatmeal, and a smoky bacon-like taste. Add a tofu scramble and you could call this breakfast.

1. Place the potatoes and ½ teaspoon of the salt in a saucepan and cover with water. Bring to a boil and cook until the potatoes are tender, approximately 8 to 10 minutes. Drain the water and press the boiled potatoes through a ricer or whip with an electric mixer. Set aside.

2. Preheat the oven to 350°F. Heat 2 tablespoons of the oil in a skillet over medium-high heat. Add the onion, mushrooms, smoked paprika, and remaining salt. Sauté for 7 to 8 minutes or until the vegetables are tender.

3. Pour in the white wine, stir, and let simmer until the liquid has been absorbed. Add the mushroom mixture to the potatoes along with the oats. Stir to combine.

4. Form into 6 patties. Heat the remaining 1 tablespoon oil over medium heat in the skillet used to sauté the vegetables. Place the patties in the skillet and cook approximately 5 minutes on each side until browned.

5. Transfer the patties to a nonstick baking sheet and bake in the oven an additional 30 minutes, flipping halfway through, or until firm.

Makes 6 burgers.

Quick Tip: This burger makes an amazing breakfast burrito. Add a crumbled burger to a flour tortilla shell. Top with some nondairy cheese and a drizzle of Ranch Dressing (page 125), roll up, and enjoy!

2 medium-size potatoes
    (red skin or white round),
    peeled and cut into chunks
1 teaspoon sea salt, divided
3 tablespoons olive oil,
    divided
1 medium onion, diced
4 portobello mushrooms,
    stems and gills removed,
    diced
2 teaspoons smoked paprika
4 tablespoons white wine
1 cup steel-cut oats, cooked

Caramelized Onion Burger

This burger is dedicated to all the onion lovers out there. Perfectly caramelized, perfectly delicious!

1 tablespoon oil

1 sweet onion, thinly sliced

1 fennel bulb, thinly sliced

2 teaspoons sea salt, divided

3 tablespoons apple cider vinegar

1 cup cooked quinoa

1½ cups mashed red potatoes, skins left on (see Quick Tip)

1. Preheat the oven to 400°F. Line a baking sheet with parchment paper or nonstick foil, and set aside.

2. Heat the olive oil in a large sauté pan over low to medium heat. Add the onion and fennel to the pan and stir to coat. Sprinkle with 1 teaspoon of salt. Cook for 5 minutes and stir, then continue to cook and stir every 5 minutes until the onions and fennel are tender and caramelized, about 40 minutes.

3. Transfer the cooked onion and fennel to a large bowl. While the pan is still hot, pour the vinegar in the pan and, along with any remaining bits and pieces of onion and fennel, add the liquid to the large bowl.

4. Add in the quinoa, potatoes, and the remaining 1 teaspoon of salt to the bowl and mix well. Form into 7 patties and place on the prepared baking sheet.

5. Bake the patties for 20 minutes, then flip them over and bake for an additional 20 minutes or until firm. Serve the burgers topped with additional caramelized onions for a more intense flavor.

Makes 7 burgers.

Quick Tip: For quick and easy mashed potatoes, bring a pot of water to a boil. Add the potatoes and cook until tender but still firm, then drain. Use a potato masher, fork, or handheld blender to whip and mash the potatoes to your desired consistency. If necessary, add a bit of nondairy milk or nondairy butter to help keep the mashed potatoes creamy and smooth. Note: One pound of potatoes yields about 2 cups mashed.

Crunchy Burger Patties

This hearty burger can satisfy even the biggest of appetites. It's as big on taste as it is on crunch—and sure to become a family favorite. These delicious burgers pair really well with our Smokey Ranch Potato Salad (page 139) and Crispy Sesame Green Bean Fries (page 144).

1. In a small bowl mix together the ground flaxseed and 3 tablespoons of lukewarm water. Let sit for 5 minutes.

2. Heat 1 tablespoon of olive oil in a large skillet over medium-high heat. Add the onions and garlic and sauté until the onions are translucent, about 3 to 4 minutes.

3. Place the oats in a blender or food processor and pulse to a flour consistency.

4. Place all of the ingredients (including the oat flour and flaxseed mixture) into a large mixing bowl and stir well. Form the mixture into 8 to 10 patties, packing the dough as firmly as possible.

5. In a skillet, heat a tablespoon or so of olive oil over medium-high heat. Cook the burger patties in batches for 5 minutes on each side. Reduce heat to medium and continue cooking for 4–5 minutes or until heated through and slightly crispy on the outside.

Makes 8–10 burgers.

Ingredients:

- 1 tablespoon ground flaxseed
- 3 tablespoons lukewarm water
- 1 tablespoon olive oil, plus extra for frying
- ½ medium onion, diced
- 2–3 cloves garlic, minced
- 1 cup old-fashioned oats
- ½ cup Homemade Bread Crumbs (page 108)
- 1 cup grated carrot (or ½ cup grated carrot and ½ cup finely chopped broccoli)
- 1 cup cooked lentils, mashed
- 1–2 tablespoons oregano
- ½ cup almonds, crushed
- ½ cup pumpkin seeds
- 2 tablespoons coconut aminos, soy sauce, or tamari (gluten-free if needed)
- 1 teaspoon chili powder
- 1 teaspoon cumin
- 1 teaspoon chopped parsley
- Sea salt and pepper to taste

Fun Fact: It's only been in recent years that flaxseed has finally gotten the recognization that it deserves. Recent studies have suggested that flaxseed may help to prevent breast cancer, prostate cancer, and colon cancer. Along with having antioxidant properties, it's high in omega-3 essential fatty acids, which have been shown to have positive heart-healthy effects. Unlike chia seeds, flaxseeds need to be ground in order for our bodies to reap the benefits. Try adding ground flaxseeds to smoothies, oatmeal, salads, and your favorite nondairy yogurt.

Sweet Potato Quinoa Burger

This is one of our most popular burger recipes, and for good reason. They are delicious, easy to make, and family-friendly. They can be baked, panfried, or even grilled—and they save really well, making them the perfect "frozen dinner." Sweet potatoes pair nicely with peanut butter, so try serving these burgers with our Peanutty Brussels Slaw (page 140) for a winning combination.

3 cups cubed sweet potatoes (about 3 regular-sized potatoes, peeled)

1¾ cups cooked black beans

¾ cup sweet corn (thaw if frozen)

½ medium red onion, finely chopped

3 cloves garlic, minced

½ cup cooked quinoa

1 tablespoon olive oil

Heaping ⅓ cup garbanzo bean flour or almond flour

2 tablespoons roasted sunflower seeds

¼ teaspoon sea salt

Fresh black pepper to taste

1 teaspoon cumin

1 teaspoon oregano

1 teaspoon chili powder

¼ teaspoon cayenne (optional)

1 tablespoon hot sauce (optional)

1. Fill a large pot ¾ full of water and bring to a boil. Add the sweet potatoes and lower the heat to simmering. Let the potatoes cook for about 15 to 20 minutes or until tender. Drain the potatoes and set aside to cool.

2. While the potatoes are cooling, preheat the oven to 375°F and line a baking sheet with parchment paper or nonstick foil. Once the potatoes have cooled, use a fork to mash them. You want them mashed but not creamy.

3. Place half of the black beans in a large mixing bowl and mash with a fork. Add the rest of the beans and the remaining ingredients including the cooked sweet potatoes. Stir until just combined.

4. Form the mixture into 10 patties and place on the prepared baking sheet. Bake for 15 minutes, then flip the burgers over and continue baking for another 15 minutes or until firm.

Makes 10 burgers.

Fun Fact: Want your skin and hair to glow? Eat a sweet potato! The combination of beta-carotene, vitamin E, and vitamin C in one food makes the sweet potato one heck of a "beauty food." These nutrients all contribute to a healthy, glowing complexion and vibrant hair.

Asian Corn Burger

This isn't your ordinary burger—more like a fritter. Crispy and crunchy on the outside, and sweet and flavorful on the inside, this "burger" is best served as is with a swipe of delicious Sweet Teriyaki Sauce (page 112).

1. In a medium bowl, mix together the flour, baking powder, chives, and salt. Add in the soy sauce, vinegar, sesame oil, and milk, and stir well. Add the corn, garlic, and ginger, and stir well until thoroughly mixed.

2. Heat a large sauté pan over medium-high heat and add enough oil to coat the bottom of the pan. Add ½ cup of the dough to the sauté pan and press down slightly (the dough should spread like a pancake, about ¼ to ½ inch thick). Repeat with the remaining dough. Panfry for about 2 minutes on each side or until crispy and golden brown.

Makes 5-6 burgers, or approximately 2 servings.

Fun Fact: There are so many negative nutrition myths about corn that its image has been seriously tarnished. Myth #1: Corn is fattening and sugary. Truth: An ear of corn has about the same number of calories as an apple and less than one-fourth the sugar. Myth #2: Cooking corn makes it less nutritious. Truth: Antioxidant activity, which helps protect the body from cancer and heart disease, is actually increased when corn is cooked. Myth #3: Corn has no health benefits. Truth: Sweet corn is loaded with lutein and zeaxanthin, two phytochemicals that promote healthy vision. Also, a mid-sized ear of corn offers a helpful three-gram dose of dietary fiber.

1½ cups garbanzo bean flour

¼ teaspoon baking powder

¼ cup finely chopped fresh chives

Sea salt to taste

4 tablespoons soy sauce, tamari, or coconut aminos (gluten-free if needed)

3 tablespoons brown rice vinegar

1 teaspoon toasted sesame oil

½ cup nondairy milk

2 cups sweet corn (thaw if frozen)

3-4 cloves garlic, minced

1 teaspoon freshly minced ginger

Olive oil or other neutral-flavor oil for frying

Happy Crabby Patty

You'll love all the crunch and flavor that this burger brings to the plate. It's our Naked Kitchen version of a crab cake. As a bonus, no crabs are harmed in the making of this burger!

1 rib celery

1 carrot

½ small onion

1 small zucchini

⅛ cup nondairy milk

¼ cup canola oil, plus 1 tablespoon for browning the patties

1 teaspoon freshly squeezed lemon juice

2 tablespoons Dijon mustard

3 teaspoons Old Bay Seasoning

1 teaspoon Worcestershire sauce (gluten-free if needed)

¼ teaspoon kelp or dulse granules

Sea salt to taste

⅛ teaspoon ground black pepper or to taste

¼ cup nutritional yeast

1 cup almond meal

¼ cup whole grain flour of your choice

Tangy Tarter Sauce (optional, page 126)

Lemon slices (optional)

1. Place the celery, carrot, onion, and zucchini in a food processor and pulse until finely chopped, or finely shred with a box grater. Transfer to a large bowl.

2. Add the milk, ¼ cup oil, lemon juice, mustard, Old Bay Seasoning, Worcestershire sauce, kelp granules, salt, and pepper to the food processor and process for 20 to 30 seconds until well mixed. Add the nutritional yeast and pulse to combine.

3. Pour the mixture into the large bowl with the vegetables. Add the almond meal and stir to combine. Add the flour and stir until mixed. Form the mixture into 6 patties (about ½ cup each).

4. Heat the remaining oil in a large nonstick skillet over medium-high heat, and cook the patties for about 5 to 7 minutes on each side until nicely browned.

5. Serve the burgers hot with Tangy Tarter Sauce (page 126) and lemon slices if desired.

Makes 6 burgers.

Quick Tip: Almond meal versus almond flour—is there a difference? Technically speaking, there is. Almond meal is made from whole, ground almonds (skin and all). Almond flour is made from blanched almonds (skins removed) and sifted to produce a finer powder. In most recipes, like this one, the two terms can be used interchangeably. If you can't find almond meal at your local food store, substitute with almond flour. You can also make your own almond meal by processing whole almonds in a food processor or coffee grinder. Homemade almond meal will keep in the fridge for up to 1 month or in the freezer for 6 months.

Seeduction Garden Burger

Seeds aren't just for the birds. This burger will seduce you with its tasty combination of nutritious seeds and flavorful garden veggies.

1. Bring 2 cups of water to a boil in a large saucepan.

2. Place the millet and quinoa in a large skillet over medium-high heat. Toast, stirring often, until slightly toasted and nutty smelling, about 3 to 5 minutes.

3. Transfer to the pan of boiling water and add ½ teaspoon of the canola oil. Cover, reduce heat, and simmer for 20 minutes or until the water has cooked off and the millet and quinoa are tender.

4. Place the carrots, kale, and onion in a food processor. Process until you have small confetti-like bits.

5. Heat 1 tablespoon of the canola oil in a skillet over medium-high heat. Add the processed vegetables and the garlic and sauté until tender. Transfer to a bowl and add the mashed sweet potato. Add the millet and quinoa, then add in the vinegar, salt, pepper, and fennel (if using).

6. Place the chia seeds in a small bowl and add 1 cup of water. Stir until you have a paste-like consistency. Add the chia paste to the bowl with the vegetables and seeds. Stir to combine. Form the mixture into 16 to 18 small patties, using approximately ½ cup of mixture per patty.

7. In a sauté pan, heat ½ tablespoon of the canola oil and ½ teaspoon of the coconut oil over medium-high heat. Place half of the burgers in the skillet and cook on each side for 10 to 15 minutes or until lightly browned and firm. Remove to a plate.

8. Add the remaining ½ tablespoon of canola oil and ½ teaspoon of coconut oil to the skillet and cook the remaining burgers.

Makes 16–18 burgers.

3 cups water, divided

½ cup millet

½ cup quinoa

2 tablespoons plus 1 teaspoon canola oil, divided

2 carrots, chopped

2 cups chopped kale

1 medium onion, chopped

2 cloves garlic, minced

1 medium sweet potato, cooked and mashed

1 tablespoon freshly squeezed lemon juice or apple cider vinegar

1 teaspoon sea salt

½ teaspoon white pepper

½ teaspoon ground fennel (optional)

⅓ cup chia seeds, ground

1 teaspoon coconut oil, divided

Fun Fact: Kale is one of the most nutritious foods on the planet. One cup of chopped kale contains 33 calories and 9 percent of the daily recommended value of calcium, 206 percent of vitamin A, 134 percent of vitamin C, and 684 percent of vitamin K. It is also a good source of potassium, iron, and phosphorus.

Curry Burger

These curry-spiced burgers are full of flavor and packed with nutrition. We like them on their own with a salad of greens, but they are equally good in a pita with a slice of tomato and a spoonful of Miso Dijonnaise (page 124).

½ cup chopped cauliflower (bite-sized pieces)

½ cup diced sweet potato

½ small onion, diced

½ red pepper, diced

1 medium carrot, diced

1 tablespoon plus 2 teaspoons canola oil, divided

1 teaspoon sea salt

1–2 cloves garlic, minced

2 teaspoons Madras curry powder (or any other Indian curry powder of your choice, to taste)

3–4 stalks curly kale, stems removed

¼ cup chia powder (aka ground chia seeds), preferably white

1 cup cooked yellow lentils

1 cup cooked brown rice

2 teaspoons coconut oil

1. Place the cauliflower, sweet potato, onion, red pepper, and carrot in a food processor and pulse into confetti-like crumbles.

2. Heat a large skillet over medium-high heat and add 1 tablespoon of the canola oil. Add the processed vegetables and sauté for 2 to 3 minutes, then add the salt and continue to cook until soft (about 4 to 6 minutes total). Add the garlic and curry powder, then continue to cook for 1 to 2 minutes more.

3. Place the kale in the food processor and pulse into confetti-like pieces. Add the kale to the skillet and cook until soft, about 2 to 3 minutes. Remove from the heat.

4. In a small bowl combine the chia powder with ½ cup of water.

5. In a large bowl combine the lentils, rice, sautéed vegetables, and the chia mixture.

6. Wipe out the skillet used to cook the vegetables and place back on medium-high heat with 1 teaspoon of canola oil and 1 teaspoon coconut oil.

7. Form half the burger mixture into 4 patties and place in the skillet. Brown each side for about 5 minutes, then lower the heat to medium-low and let cook about 10 minutes more on each side until crispy and golden on the outside and soft and warm on the inside.

8. Add the remaining canola and coconut oil to the skillet and repeat with the last of the burger mixture.

Makes 8 burgers.

Quick Tip: Madras curry or Madras sauce is a fairly hot curry sauce, red in color and with heavy use of chili powder. If you are unable to find Madras curry powder in your local grocery store, you can substitute it with any other Indian curry powder of your choice.

Baked Broccoli Burger

Think you don't like broccoli? Think again! The flavor of broccoli changes when it's steamed or roasted, and in this burger you would never know the healthy green was added in. Broccoli never tasted so good, and even the pickiest of eaters will enjoy this!

1. Preheat the oven to 400°F. Line a baking sheet with parchment paper or nonstick foil, and set aside.

2. In a small pot, bring 1 cup of water and the couscous to a boil. Remove from heat immediately and allow the couscous to sit in the pot for 10 minutes, soaking up the water.

3. While the couscous rests, heat the safflower oil in a nonstick skillet over medium-high heat. Add the yellow onion, green onion, and garlic. Sauté for 3 to 5 minutes or until the onions are soft and translucent. Remove from heat and let cool for 5 minutes.

4. Transfer the onions and garlic to a food processor and add the couscous, broccoli, garbanzo beans, tahini, cumin, lemon juice, and sea salt.

5. Pulse the mixture 3 or 4 times, stopping to scrape down the sides if necessary, and then transfer to a large mixing bowl. Add the bread crumbs and gently mix until well incorporated.

6. Form the mixture into 8 patties and place on the prepared baking sheet. Bake for 20 minutes, flip the burgers over, and bake for an additional 20 minutes or until firm.

Makes 8 burgers.

Fun Fact: The next time you have a cold, skip the glass of orange juice and pick up a piece of broccoli. Just 1 cup of chopped broccoli has the same amount of vitamin C as one orange. Broccoli is also very high in vitamin A, which helps fight cancer within your cells and keeps your eyes healthy, staving off glaucoma and other degenerative eye diseases. It also helps to promote healthy skin, break down urinary stones, and maintains healthy bones and teeth.

⅓ cup dry whole-wheat couscous

1 tablespoon safflower oil or other neutral-flavor oil

½ cup diced yellow onion

½ cup chopped green onion

1 clove garlic, minced

1½ cups broccoli florets, steamed

1¾ cups cooked garbanzo beans

1 tablespoon tahini

1–2 teaspoons cumin

1 tablespoon freshly squeezed lemon juice

1 teaspoon sea salt

½ cup Homemade Bread Crumbs (page 108)

Spoon Burger

Why a Spoon Burger? Cause you won't want to miss a bite and you will need a spoon to get every little bit that falls on your plate!

8-ounce package tempeh

2 tablespoons coconut aminos, soy sauce, or tamari (gluten-free if needed)

2 tablespoons olive oil, divided

2 carrots, finely chopped

1 medium onion, finely chopped

1 rib celery, finely chopped

2 cloves garlic, minced

1 teaspoon sea salt or to taste

6–7 ounces no-salt-added tomato paste

1 teaspoon paprika

1 teaspoon dry mustard

½ cup ketchup

2 tablespoons apple butter

2 tablespoons apple cider vinegar

2 tablespoons coconut crystals or other dry sweetener of your choice

1 teaspoon Worcestershire sauce (gluten-free if needed)

¼ cup low-sodium vegetable broth

2 tablespoons nutritional yeast

1. Break the tempeh into crumbles in a small bowl and add in the coconut aminos. Let sit for 2–3 minutes.

2. Heat a nonstick skillet over medium-high heat and add 1 tablespoon of the oil. Transfer the tempeh to the skillet and fry, stirring often until slightly browned. Transfer back into the bowl.

3. Place the skillet over medium-high heat and add the remaining 1 tablespoon of oil. Add the carrot, onion, celery, garlic, and salt. Sauté the vegetables until tender, about 4 minutes.

4. Add the tomato paste and mix well, stirring frequently until the tomato paste has caramelized into a rich dark-red color. Stir in the paprika and dry mustard. Stir in the ketchup, apple butter, vinegar, coconut crystals, Worcestershire sauce, vegetable broth, and nutritional yeast.

5. Add the browned tempeh and mix well, adding more vegetable broth if a thinner consistency is desired. Simmer until hot and bubbly and serve over toasted sandwich buns.

Makes 4 large or 6 smaller sandwiches.

Fun Fact: Tempeh is made from cooked and slightly fermented soybeans and formed into a rectangular patty. Tempeh is a probiotic food, which means it contains bacteria that our bodies need to stay healthy. It is a complete protein, containing all nine essential amino acids, and has soy isoflavones that strengthen bones, help to ease menopausal symptoms, and reduce the risk of coronary heart disease and some cancers.

Roasted Eggplant Patty

Eggplant is an ideal ingredient in veggie burgers. It works as a binder to hold the ingredients together and lends itself well to other flavors, as in this Greek-inspired burger. Serve with a side of Fava Beans with Peppers and Tomatoes (page 165) and Homemade Pita Bread (page 94) for a wonderfully satisfying meal.

1. Preheat the oven to 350°F.

2. Toss the eggplants and mushrooms with 3 tablespoons of oil and ½ teaspoon of salt. Arrange the vegetables in a single layer on a baking sheet (use more than one baking sheet if necessary; the vegetables should not overlap or they will retain too much moisture) and roast for 40 to 45 minutes, or until lightly browned.

3. Place the walnuts in a food processor and pulse until finely ground. Add the eggplant, the mushrooms, and the remaining ingredients, except the remaining tablespoon of oil, and process until completely ground and the mixture holds together. Taste and add additional salt and pepper if desired.

4. Form the mixture into 6 to 8 patties. Heat the remaining 1 tablespoon of oil in a large skillet over medium-high heat. Cook the patties for about 5 minutes on each side until nicely browned.

Makes 6–8 burgers.

Fun Fact: Are you stressed? Try eating an eggplant! Eggplants are high in bioflavonoids, which are known to control high blood pressure and relieve stress. Regular consumption of eggplant also helps to prevent blood clots—thanks again to bioflavonoids and vitamin K, which strengthen capillaries.

- 2 medium eggplants, peeled and cubed
- 8 ounces (approximately 16) cremini mushrooms, halved
- 4 tablespoons olive oil, divided
- 1 teaspoon sea salt, divided
- ¼ cup walnuts
- ¼ cup unseasoned, toasted bread crumbs (gluten-free if needed)
- 1 tablespoon tahini
- 1 tablespoon lemon zest
- 1 teaspoon lemon juice
- 1 teaspoon onion powder
- ½ teaspoon garlic powder
- ½ teaspoon oregano
- ½ teaspoon marjoram
- ¼ teaspoon black pepper or to taste

Broccoli Cheese Casserole Burger

Remember that classic broccoli casserole? This is a play on that casserole in the form of a delicious and healthy burger. We like to pair this burger with our Crunchy Baked Onion Rings (page 158) or a fresh green salad.

½ cup roasted almonds

½ cup crushed brown rice crackers

2 cups small broccoli florets

½ cup diced yellow onion

8–10 medium-sized cremini mushrooms, diced (approximately 1 cup)

1 tablespoon plus 1 teaspoon olive oil, divided

½ teaspoon salt

1 cup shredded nondairy cheddar cheese

¼ cup powdered soy milk

2 tablespoons tamari or soy sauce (gluten-free if needed)

1. Place the almonds in a food processor and process until ground. Transfer to a large bowl and add the crushed rice crackers.

2. Place the broccoli and onion in the food processor and pulse until coarsely ground. Add the mushrooms and pulse until no large pieces remain.

3. Heat 1 tablespoon of oil in a large nonstick skillet over medium high-heat. Add the ground vegetables to the skillet. Add the salt and cook for 5 to 6 minutes until tender.

4. Turn off the heat and immediately add the cheese so it starts to melt (this will help the burgers hold together when forming into patties).

5. Transfer the mixture to the bowl with the crackers and almonds. Add the powdered soy milk and soy sauce and stir to combine.

6. Wipe out the skillet used to cook the vegetables and heat the remaining 1 teaspoon of oil over medium to medium-low heat.

7. To form the patties, take approximately ½ cup of the burger mixture at a time and compress it tightly into a ball in your hands. Flatten and place in the skillet.

8. Cook slowly over medium to medium-low heat so that the burgers brown but the cheese doesn't burn, approximately 5 minutes on each side.

Makes 6 burgers.

Quick Tip: Brown rice crackers are a favorite snack of ours, and in this recipe their fun, crunchy texture takes the place of ordinary bread crumbs. Our favorite brand of brown rice crackers is Edward & Sons Organic Brown Rice Snaps. If this product is not available in your local food store, select a product that lists organic brown rice flour, organic white rice flour, or a combination of both as its only ingredient.

Spicy Veggie Falafel Burger

These flavorful burgers are bursting with nutrients. Vitamin- and mineral-rich carrots, cauliflower, garlic, and parsley pair well with omega-filled chia seeds and almonds. This time you can feel good about going back for seconds!

1. In a small bowl, combine the chia seeds with the boiling water and stir until well combined. Let stand for a few minutes to thicken.

2. Process the almonds in a food processor or blender to a sand-like consistency. Add the cauliflower, carrots, onion, garlic, and parsley. Pulse a few times until the mixture is coarsely chopped.

3. Add the lemon juice, cumin, soy sauce, and cayenne. Pulse once or twice to combine.

4. Transfer the mixture to a large bowl and add in the chia seed mixture. Stir well until thoroughly combined.

5. In ¼ cup increments add in the flour until your burger mixtures holds together when formed. Form the burger mixture into 12 patties.

6. Heat a small amount of oil in a large nonstick sauté pan. Working in batches, panfry the patties for about 3 to 4 minutes on each side or until they are lightly browned.

Makes 12 burgers.

- 2 tablespoons chia seeds or ground flaxseed
- 6 tablespoons boiling water
- 1 cup almonds (raw or roasted)
- 1 cup cauliflower florets
- 1 cup chopped carrots
- 1 small red onion
- 1–2 cloves garlic, peeled
- 1 cup fresh parsley leaves
- 1 tablespoon freshly squeezed lemon juice
- 1½ teaspoons cumin
- 1 teaspoon soy sauce, tamari, or coconut aminos (gluten-free if needed)
- ½ teaspoon cayenne
- ½–¾ cup garbanzo bean flour
- Small amount of olive oil for frying

Fun Fact: Chia seeds may be tiny but their benefits are huge! Chia seeds are a balanced blend of protein, carbohydrates, fats, and fiber. It is said that 1 tablespoon of chia can sustain a person for twenty-four hours. Along with being an excellent source of omega-3 fatty acid, they also boast 10 grams of fiber per 2 tablespoons while providing iron, calcium, magnesium, zinc, and protein.

Breakfast Omelet Burger

Do you ever crave breakfast food in the evening? If so, this recipe is for you. Morning or evening, serve this burger on toasted English Muffins (page 97) alongside roasted potatoes and a big glass of orange juice. If you have it for dinner, make enough to save for breakfast the next day!

1 cup garbanzo bean flour

¾–1 cup water

3 tablespoons olive oil or other neutral-flavor oil

2 tablespoons nutritional yeast

1 teaspoon ground mustard

1 teaspoon sea salt

½ teaspoon garlic powder

½ teaspoon mixed dried herbs (parsley, rosemary, and oregano work great)

2 cups finely diced veggies of your choice (red pepper, asparagus, mushrooms, onions, broccoli, and zucchini are great options)

1. Preheat the oven to 350°F. Lightly grease a 6-count 4-inch baking tin or other tin of your choice (you can make these burgers in any size that baking tins come in) and set aside.

2. In a large bowl mix together the flour, water, oil, nutritional yeast, mustard, salt, garlic powder, and herbs. Then add in the veggies and gently fold to combine.

3. Pour the batter evenly into your prepared tin and bake for approximately 25 minutes until the tops are lightly brown and the centers bounce back when pressed upon. Remove the tin from the oven and let cool for about 5 minutes.

4. To remove the individual omelets, flip the tin over on a solid work surface and gently tap the back; they should fall right out. Serve on an English Muffin and top with mashed avocado, sprouts, or some Roasted Tomato Ketchup (page 106).

Makes 4–6 burgers.

Quick Tip: If you don't have a baking tin or just want to serve this dish as a traditional omelet, simply pour the entire batter into a nonstick skillet over medium heat. Cook until the edges start to brown, 5 to 10 minutes, then flip the omelet over and continue to cook for another 4 to 5 minutes, or until golden brown. Cut into wedges or fold in half and serve.

Kraut Burger Bundles

Our ancestors were part of a group of immigrants called Germans from Russia. We grew up eating many of the traditional foods of their culture, and a favorite was something called Kraut Berok. Typically Kraut Berok was made with ground meat. This adaptation uses earthy cremini mushrooms ground to a meat-like crumble. Tradition successfully updated!

1. Preheat the oven to 350°F. Line 2 baking sheets with parchment or silicone mats.

2. Heat 2 tablespoons of the oil in a large pot over medium-high heat. Add the onion, fennel, and 1 teaspoon of the salt. Cook until softened, about 5 minutes.

3. Add the mushrooms and cook for 4 to 5 minutes until most of the moisture has cooked off.

4. Add the cabbage, black pepper, and the remaining salt. Add remaining oil if needed. Reduce the heat to medium and cook for 8 to 10 minutes or until the cabbage is tender and translucent. Turn off the heat, cover, and keep warm.

5. On a floured surface, roll out the dough into a rectangle to a ¼-inch thickness. Cut the dough into approximately 12 five-inch squares.

6. Spoon about 3 tablespoons of the cabbage filling into the center of each square. Pull up each corner of the dough to the center and pinch to close. Pinch all along the seams to seal. Place the bundle sealed side down onto a baking sheet. Repeat with remaining dough and filling, placing the bundles so they don't touch on the baking sheets.

7. Bake for 18 to 20 minutes or until the bread is lightly browned at the edges.

Store in an airtight container in the refrigerator for 3 to 4 days, or in a freezer-safe container in the freezer for up to 1 month.

Makes approximately 12 bundles.

- 2–3 tablespoons canola oil or other neutral-flavor oil
- 1 medium yellow onion, diced
- ½ cup thinly sliced fennel
- 2 teaspoons sea salt
- 6 ounces cremini mushrooms, very finely chopped or processed
- 2 cups shredded cabbage
- 1 teaspoon black pepper or to taste
- **Dough from Whole-Wheat Hamburger Buns (page 90) or your favorite bread dough recipe equivalent for 1 loaf**

Miso-Marinated Portobello Burger

We love a good portobello burger, and this Asian-inspired burger is one of our absolute favorites. It's delicious as a traditional burger or sliced and served with your favorite rice, pasta, or salad.

2 tablespoons sweet white miso

2 tablespoons coconut crystals, coconut nectar, honey, or brown rice syrup

1 tablespoon soy sauce or tamari (gluten-free if needed)

3 tablespoons olive oil

2 tablespoons freshly squeezed lemon juice

4 portobello mushrooms, stems and gills removed

1. Combine the miso, coconut crystals, soy sauce, olive oil, and lemon juice in a medium-sized bowl and whisk to combine.

2. Rub the marinade evenly over the mushrooms. Place them in a resealable bag with the remaining marinade. Place in the refrigerator for at least 1 hour or up to overnight.

3. Preheat the oven to 350°F.

4. Remove the mushrooms from the marinade and transfer, gill side down, to a foil- or parchment-lined baking sheet.

5. Bake for 30 minutes or until the mushrooms are dry on top and tender throughout.

Makes 4 burgers.

Quick Tip: These mushrooms are also great prepared on the grill. Place the marinated mushrooms on a sheet of foil in the center of your grill. Cook for about 10 minutes on high heat or until the burgers are tender throughout.

BURGER BUNS

Whole-Wheat Hamburger Buns

This burger bun is the best bun for almost any burger. It's soft and tender with just a little hint of sweetness. So good you might want to make a few extra for breakfast the next day.

2 tablespoons coconut nectar, honey, or brown rice syrup

1¼ cups warm water (about 110°F)

1 tablespoon active dry yeast

3–3½ cups hard white whole-wheat flour

2 tablespoons soy milk powder

½ teaspoon fine sea salt

1 tablespoon olive or canola oil, plus a little more to spray the bowl when raising the dough and for the baking pan

1 tablespoon apple cider vinegar

Quick Tip: This recipe is very versatile, so don't stop at just making hamburger buns. Try shaping your dough into a standard bread loaf; spread it thin to make a pizza crust; or create cinnamon rolls by rolling it flat, top with a layer of nondairy butter and sprinkle with cinnamon and coconut crystals, then roll it up and bake in the oven until golden brown.

1. Place the coconut nectar in a large bowl. Add the warm water and stir to combine. Sprinkle the yeast evenly over the top and let sit for 5 to 10 minutes or until a foam has settled on the top of the water.

2. Add in 2 cups of the flour, soy milk powder, salt, oil, and vinegar. Stir to combine. Then add in 1 cup more of the flour and mix until you have a dough that is workable for kneading (not too sticky). Add another ½ cup if needed.

3. Knead the dough for 10 to 15 minutes by hand, or for approximately 7 to 8 minutes in a stand mixer with a dough hook. The dough should be smooth and elastic.

4. Spray the bowl used to mix the dough with a little oil and place the ball of dough in the bowl. Cover with wax paper and place in a warm area to rise, until the dough is doubled. This dough rises quite fast so it will only take about an hour.

5. Shape into balls about 3 to 4 inches in diameter. Place on a baking sheet that has been lightly sprayed with oil, cover, and let rise for another 20 to 30 minutes.

6. Preheat the oven to 350°F. Bake the buns for 10 to 14 minutes or until lightly browned.

7. Remove from the oven and let cool before slicing.

Store at room temperature in an airtight container for up to 2 days.

Makes 8 hamburger buns.

Potato Onion Bread and Buns

This hearty bread is perfect as a side for salads and soups and can also be made into hamburger buns to accompany your favorite burger.

1. In a large bowl, combine ½ cup of the water and the coconut nectar. Once the coconut nectar is completely dissolved, sprinkle the yeast on top and let stand for 10 minutes.

2. Add in the remaining 1½ cups of water and the rest of the ingredients except the oil. Mix well until all the ingredients are thoroughly combined.

3. Remove the dough from the bowl and place on a lightly floured work surface. Gently knead the dough for about 6 to 7 minutes. Shape your dough into a ball and set aside.

4. Coat your bowl with oil and place your dough ball into the bowl. Cover with a damp kitchen towel and place in a warm area to rise for 1 hour.

5. Rub a little oil on a baking sheet and set aside. Shape your dough into 2 loaves or 12 to 14 hamburger buns. Cover again with your damp kitchen towel and let the dough rise for another 30 minutes.

6. Preheat the oven to 400°F. Bake in the oven for 22 to 25 minutes for loaves, or for 12 to 15 minutes for buns. Remove the bread from the oven and let cool on a baking rack before slicing.

Store at room temperature in an airtight container for up to 2 days.

Makes 2 loaves, or 12–14 hamburger buns.

2 cups warm water, divided (about 110°F)

1 teaspoon coconut nectar, honey, or brown rice syrup

2¼ teaspoons dry yeast

1 teaspoon sea salt

1 cup mashed potatoes (any type of white potato will work)

2½ cups spelt flour, plus a little extra for dusting your work surface

2 cups whole-wheat pastry flour

3½ tablespoons minced onion

1 tablespoon olive oil

Homemade Pita Bread

One of my favorite ways to eat a burger is inside a pita with lots of yummy vegetables stuffed inside. This recipe is so simple, and once you make homemade pita bread you'll never go back to the store-bought variety again!

1¼ cups warm water (about 110°F)

1 tablespoon coconut nectar, honey, or brown rice syrup

2¼ teaspoons active dry yeast

3 cups whole-wheat pastry flour

1½ teaspoons sea salt

2 tablespoons extra-virgin olive oil, divided

1. In a large bowl, combine ½ cup of the water and the coconut nectar. Once the coconut nectar is completely dissolved, sprinkle the yeast on top and let stand for 10 minutes.

2. Add the flour, salt, the remaining ¾ cup of water, and 1½ tablespoons of the oil to the bowl and mix well. Form into a ball.

3. Place the ball on a work surface, adding a bit of flour if needed, and knead the dough for about 10 minutes. Use the remaining ½ tablespoon of oil to lightly coat your bowl and place the dough back in it. Cover the bowl with plastic wrap or a damp kitchen towel and set aside to rise until it has doubled in size, about 90 minutes.

4. Remove the dough from the bowl and divide into 8 pieces. Form each piece into a ball and place on a baking sheet. Cover with a damp towel and let rest for 20 minutes.

5. Preheat the oven to 400°F. After the dough has rested, spread a light coating of flour on your work surface and place one of the balls of dough there. Sprinkle a little flour on top of it and, using a rolling pin or your hands, stretch and flatten the dough. You should be able to roll it out to ⅛ to ¼ inch thick. Repeat with the remaining balls of dough.

6. Place as many pitas as you can fit onto a hot baking stone or pan and bake in the oven for 3 minutes. Depending on the type of flour used, they may or may not be puffy inside.

7. Remove from oven and repeat with the remaining pita dough.

Store at room temperature in an airtight container for up to 2 days.

Makes 8 pitas.

Quick Tip: Want to change up your pita? Try these variations for a fun twist:

1½ cups millet flour and 1½ cups whole-wheat pastry flour = a hint of corn

1½ cups barley flour and 1½ cups whole-wheat pastry flour = buttery biscuit flavor

1½ cups spelt flour and 1½ cups whole-wheat pastry flour = country bread flavor

English Muffins

English muffins aren't just for breakfast—they make great buns, too. For those times when you want a little less bun so that the scrumptious burger can be the star of the show, these crumpet-style English muffins are the perfect choice.

1. In a bowl, combine the water and the maple syrup. Stir until the maple syrup is dissolved. Sprinkle the yeast over the top and let sit for about 5 minutes until foamy.

2. In a separate bowl, combine the flour, starch, salt, and baking powder. Add the milk and yeast mixture and beat briskly for a couple of minutes, until you have a thick pancake batter. Cover and let rise until it's puffed up and bubbly, about 1 hour.

3. Heat a nonstick grill pan on low heat, and grease the pan as well as 14 to 16 muffin rings. Place the rings on the grill and spoon in about a ¼ cup or so of the batter into each ring, filling each about halfway up. Cook for 5 to 7 minutes or until you see bubbles appear on the top and the sides start to look dry.

4. Carefully lift and twist off each ring. Flip the muffins over and cook another 5 to 7 minutes or until the insides are completely cooked and the outsides are nicely browned. (You want to cook the muffins slowly so the insides get done and aren't doughy.)

5. Let the muffins cool. Split each one by perforating all around the edges with a fork and separating it into a nice, thin bun for the burger of your choice.

Store at room temperature in an airtight container for up to 2 days.

Makes 14–16 muffins.

Quick Tip: For a kid-friendly meal that is ready in minutes, slice your English muffins in half, spread with pizza sauce, and top with nondairy cheese and your choice of toppings. Place in a preheated oven at 350°F and bake until the cheese has melted and is golden brown, about 5 to 7 minutes.

1½ cups warm water (about 110°F)

1 tablespoon maple syrup

2¼ teaspoons active dry yeast

2 cups hard white whole-wheat flour

½ cup potato starch

1 teaspoon salt

1 teaspoon baking powder

½ cup unsweetened soy milk, warmed

Canola or other neutral-flavor oil for greasing the grill pan and the muffin rings

Roasted Garlic and Herb Flatbread

The first thing you will notice when you bite into a piece of this fragrant flatbread will be how it melts in your mouth. Then the flavors will awaken your taste buds with the sweet, nutty, caramelized zing of the garlic and the wow factor of the herbs. It's the perfect complement to those burgers that don't really need a bun.

2 cups white whole-wheat
  flour
2 teaspoons baking powder
1 teaspoon garlic powder
  (not garlic salt)
½ teaspoon rosemary, ground
½ teaspoon oregano
½ teaspoon marjoram
½ teaspoon onion powder
  (not onion salt)
½ teaspoon sea salt
½ cup water
⅓ cup olive oil
1 bulb roasted garlic, mashed
  into a paste
Coarse sea salt (optional)

1. Preheat the oven to 425°F.

2. In a large bowl mix together the first 8 ingredients. Stir in the water, oil, and mashed garlic. Knead for 1 to 2 minutes until all the flour is mixed in and you have a soft dough.

3. Divide the dough into 4 equal pieces and form into balls. Roll each ball into a 6-inch disc on a piece of parchment paper that is oven-safe up to 425°F. Place the dough discs and paper onto two baking sheets (you should be able to fit 2 on each baking sheet), sprinkle with coarse sea salt if desired, and bake for 8 to 10 minutes or until golden brown.

Store at room temperature in an airtight container for up to 2 days.

Makes 4 servings.

Quick Tip: To reheat the flatbread, place it directly on your oven rack at 350°F until warm and crispy, about 3 to 5 minutes.

Herbed Socca

Socca is one of our favorite gluten-free breads. It's perfect as a burger bun, a pizza crust, or a sandwich bread.

1. Preheat the oven to 375°F. Line the bottom and sides of a large baking sheet with parchment paper. If you don't have parchment, just grease the entire pan.

2. In a large mixing bowl, whisk together all of the ingredients until smooth. Let the mixture sit for 5 to 10 minutes.

3. Pour the mixture into the pan and bake for 40 minutes or until cracked on the top with browned edges.

4. Let the bread cool for 5 minutes and then remove from the pan. Serve as is or use a knife to slice into pieces.

Store in a tightly sealed container at room temperature for 2 to 3 days.

Makes 4–6 servings.

Quick Tip: The amount of water and oil can be adjusted slightly to vary the thickness of the socca. For a thinner bread, add another ¼ to ½ cup water and an additional tablespoon of oil.

- 1¾ cups garbanzo bean flour
- 1 cup water
- 2 tablespoons olive oil or other neutral-flavor oil
- ½ teaspoon sea salt
- ½ teaspoon garlic powder
- 1½ teaspoons oregano
- 1 teaspoon parsley
- ½ teaspoon basil
- 1 teaspoon rosemary
- Black pepper to taste

Savory Corn Cakes

Sometimes a burger calls for something a little different than a basic bun. We love using these crispy corn cakes as a platform for many different burgers—especially the Zesty Bean Burgers (page 12), Southwestern Mini Sliders (page 14), Cheesy Burrito Burgers (page 21), and Buffalo Black Bean Burgers (page 33). They are also great served with Chuckwagon Beans (page 147) or topped with the chili cheese sauce from the Chili Cheese Fries recipe (page 188).

1 cup unsweetened soy milk
   or other nondairy milk
½ teaspoon cider vinegar
1 tablespoon plus 2
   teaspoons canola oil,
   divided
1 tablespoon maple syrup
½ cup yellow cornmeal
½ cup white whole-wheat
   flour or whole-wheat
   pastry flour
2 tablespoons potato starch
1 tablespoon tapioca starch
   or corn starch
1 teaspoon baking powder
½ teaspoon baking soda
½ teaspoon sea salt
½ teaspoon thyme
¼ teaspoon rosemary

1. In a small bowl, whisk together the soy milk, vinegar, 1 tablespoon oil, and maple syrup.

2. In a separate bowl, mix the cornmeal, flour, potato starch, tapioca starch, baking powder, baking soda, sea salt, thyme, and rosemary. Add the wet ingredients from the previous step and mix until combined.

3. Heat a nonstick skillet over medium heat. Coat the skillet with 1 teaspoon of the oil. Grease 6 muffin rings with the remaining teaspoon of oil.

4. Place the rings on the skillet and pour in the batter, evenly dividing the batter amongst them. Cook 4 to 5 minutes or until the cake is firm to the touch. Flip over with tongs, pressing the cake down to the bottom of the ring, and cook for an additional 4 minutes or until firm and lightly browned.

5. Run a sharp knife around the outside of the rings and remove the rings with tongs. Cool the cakes on a wire rack before serving.

Store in a tightly sealed container at room temperature for 2 to 3 days.

Makes 6 cakes.

Quick Tip: Add a fun twist to your corn cakes with these simple modifications:

Asian Corn Cakes: Omit the rosemary and thyme and add 1 teaspoon sesame oil, 1 tablespoon soy sauce, 2 tablespoons thinly sliced green onions, and 1 clove minced garlic.

Mexican Corn Cakes: Omit the rosemary and add 1 teaspoon chili powder, ½ teaspoon cumin, and a pinch of cinnamon.

CONDIMENTS AND TOPPINGS

Roasted Tomato Ketchup

This ketchup is so delicious that you'll find yourself looking for any excuse to add it to your meals. The roasted tomatoes add a slightly sweet flavor while the apple cider vinegar adds just the right amount of tang.

10 medium-sized tomatoes, halved

2 tablespoons extra-virgin olive oil, divided

Pinch of sea salt

½ large onion, finely diced

1 clove garlic, finely minced

3 tablespoons apple cider vinegar

2½ tablespoons coconut crystals or other dry sweetener of your choice

⅛ teaspoon cinnamon

⅛ teaspoon allspice

2 tablespoons coconut nectar, honey, or brown rice syrup

Freshly ground pepper to taste

1. Preheat the oven to 350°F.

2. Place each tomato half on a parchment-lined baking sheet. Lightly drizzle with 1 tablespoon of oil and a pinch of sea salt. Roast for 30 minutes or so, until the tomatoes are caramelized and fragrant.

3. Heat the remaining 1 tablespoon of olive oil in a medium-sized saucepan over medium heat. Add the onion and sauté until translucent, about 3 to 4 minutes. Transfer the onions and roasted tomatoes to a food processor or blender and process until smooth.

4. Using the back of a wooden spoon or spatula, press the tomato puree through a mesh sieve back into the saucepan. Discard any remaining pulp.

5. Add the remaining ingredients to the tomato puree and continue cooking, uncovered, stirring occasionally, for about 20 minutes until thick.

Store in an airtight container in the refrigerator for up to 2 weeks.

Makes 2 cups.

Fun Fact: Tomatoes contain important anti-inflammatory nutrients called carotenoids and bioflavonoids. The absorption of these nutrients is greater from cooked tomatoes than fresh tomatoes, since cooking breaks down the tomato cell matrix and makes the carotenoids more available. Adding olive oil to diced tomatoes during cooking greatly increases the absorption of lycopene, which has been shown to reduce the risk of cancer, particularly prostate cancer in men.

Homemade Bread Crumbs

You'll find that many of our recipes call for our Homemade Bread Crumbs. They not only add flavor but act as a binder and provide texture to our veggie burgers. Along with being an integral ingredient of the burgers themselves, they have many other uses. Sprinkle them on salads as a tasty alternative to croutons, or add them to soups, baked potatoes, and pasta dishes for extra flavor and texture.

10 pieces bread of your choice (gluten-free if needed)

¼ cup olive oil

10 heaping tablespoons nutritional yeast

2 tablespoons garlic salt (for a salt-free version substitute with garlic powder)

1 tablespoon onion powder

1 tablespoon oregano

1. Preheat the oven to 350°F.

2. Place the bread in a single layer on a baking sheet. Drizzle the olive oil over the bread and place in the oven for 5 minutes. Flip the slices over and bake for another 5 minutes or until golden brown and crispy.

3. Remove from the oven and let the bread cool completely.

4. Once the bread is cool, place in a large plastic bag and, using a rolling pin or meat tenderizer, crush the pieces of bread until you have a fine bread crumb-like consistency. (Alternatively, you can crush your bread in a food processor. Add one or two pieces to your processor at a time and pulse until you have a fine bread crumb–like consistency. Just make sure not to overprocess.)

5. Transfer the mixture to a large bowl and add in the remaining ingredients. Stir well.

Store in an airtight container in the refrigerator for up to 1 month.

Makes 4–5 cups.

Quick Tip: To make unseasoned bread crumbs, simply omit the nutritional yeast, garlic salt, onion powder, and oregano.

Sweet Heat Chili Sauce

Store-bought chili sauces tend to contain large amounts of sugar along with unnecessary fillers and preservatives. We've eliminated all those harmful ingredients and created a chili sauce with just the right amount of sweetness, a kick of heat, and a ton of flavor!

1. Place the anchos and broth in a small pan and bring to a boil. Cover and remove from heat.

2. Heat a skillet over medium heat and add the olive oil. Add the onion and carrot and cook for 8 to 10 minutes or until the onions are soft.

3. Turn heat to low and add the garlic and continue cooking 2 to 3 minutes just until the onions start to turn a light caramel color.

4. Stir in the Worcestershire sauce and tomato paste and let simmer for another 2 to 3 minutes.

5. Place the anchos with the stock into a food processor along with the onion mixture. Process until smooth. Add the molasses and pulse once or twice to mix. Add salt to taste.

Store in an airtight container in the refrigerator for up to 2 weeks.

Makes 2½ cups.

Quick Tip: This chili sauce has a wide variety of uses, so we tend to make 2 or 3 batches at a time. For long-term storage of your chili sauce (up to 1 year), fill an ice cube tray with sauce and place in the freezer. Remove the frozen chili cubes and place in a freezer-safe ziplock bag until ready to use. You can thaw your cubes at room temperature in about an hour or in the microwave in about 30 seconds.

2–3 large dried ancho peppers, stemmed and seeded

1½ cups low-sodium vegetable broth

2 tablespoons olive oil

1 large sweet onion, sliced

1 carrot, diced

2 cloves garlic, minced

1 tablespoon Worcestershire sauce (gluten-free if needed)

2 tablespoons tomato paste

2–4 tablespoons molasses (depending on how sweet you like your sauce)

Sea salt to taste

Sweet Teriyaki Sauce

The possibilities are endless with this amazing sauce. Add it to fried rice, stir-fries, and pastas, or use it as a salad dressing or a dipping sauce. Just make sure to make a double batch because it won't last long!

½ cup reduced-sodium soy sauce, tamari, or coconut aminos

2 tablespoons toasted sesame oil

2 tablespoons brown rice vinegar

2 teaspoons coconut nectar, honey, or brown rice syrup

1 whole green onion, thinly sliced

1 teaspoon minced ginger

Place all the ingredients in a bowl and mix well. Store in an airtight container in the refrigerator for up to 2 weeks.

Makes approximately ¾ cup.

Pineapple Relish

While this relish pairs well with our Caribbean Spinach Burger (page 36), you'll find that it's an excellent topping for just about any burger. Its sweet and savory flavors also make it an ideal topping on veggie dogs, baked potatoes, and salads.

Toss all of the ingredients together in a small bowl. Let sit 10 to 15 minutes before serving.

Store in an airtight container in the refrigerator for 3 to 4 days.

Makes approximately 1½ cups.

1 cup diced fresh pineapple
½ cup diced red onion
3–4 tablespoons diced red bell pepper
½ teaspoon minced fresh ginger
Juice of half a lime
½ teaspoon sea salt or to taste

Fun Fact: Feeling airsick or nauseous? Chew on some ginger. Upset stomach or painful gas? Munch on a piece of ginger. Do you have joint pain or aching muscles? Add a few pieces of ginger to a hot bath. Suffering a sore throat and nasal congestion? Sip on some ginger tea. Ginger is an herb that is widely considered to hold medical health benefits and to cure a variety of ailments. If you're looking to add more ginger to your diet, try tossing some minced ginger in with your favorite stir-fry, roasted vegetables, or fruit smoothie.

Sweet Roasted Garlic Mustard

If you've never made your own mustard, then you're in for a real treat. The flavors and textures are unlike anything you will find in a store-bought brand. Just remember, it takes about 2 to 3 weeks for the flavors to blend together, so plan ahead.

½ cup plus 1 tablespoon whole yellow mustard seeds

3 tablespoons whole brown mustard seeds

½ cup plus 2 tablespoons apple cider vinegar

¼ cup white wine

3 tablespoons water

1 head of garlic

Small amount of olive oil

1 cup maple syrup

2 teaspoons sea salt

1. Combine the mustard seeds, vinegar, wine, and water. Let stand at room temperature for about 6 hours (or overnight) or until all the liquid is absorbed.

2. Preheat the oven to 400°F. Slice off the top of the garlic head and rub it with some olive oil. Wrap the garlic in foil and roast until soft, about 30 to 40 minutes. Remove from oven and let cool. Once completely cooled, gently pop each clove of garlic from the head.

3. Combine the soaked seeds, roasted garlic, maple syrup, and salt in a food processor or blender. Pulse until the mixture resembles a grainy mustard or process for longer until you reach your desired consistency. Add a little more wine or water if your mustard is too thick.

4. Spoon the mustard into an airtight container and refrigerate for 2 to 3 weeks before use. The strong, pungent flavors of the mustard will mellow with time.

Continue to store your mustard in the refrigerator for up to 1 year.

Makes just over 2 cups.

Fun Fact: The next time you feel a case of the sniffles coming on, grab a jar of mustard! Mustard seeds are high in selenium and magnesium, and both components give it a unique anti-inflammatory property. Consumed regularly, mustard is known to control and keep the symptoms of asthma, cold, and chest congestion at bay.

Homemade Pickles

Once you go homemade, you'll never go back to store-bought again. Making your own pickles is so simple and easy you'll wonder why you didn't do it sooner!

Classic Crunch Pickles

12 ounces pickling cucumbers (2–3 cucumbers)

6 sprigs of fresh dill

1 tablespoon whole coriander seeds

½ tablespoon whole mustard seeds

1 tablespoon sea salt

¾ cup distilled white vinegar

1 tablespoon whole peppercorns

2 cloves garlic, chopped

Tangy Garlic Pickles

12 ounces pickling cucumbers (2–3 cucumbers)

¾ cup apple cider vinegar

6 cloves garlic, chopped

1 tablespoon whole peppercorns

1 tablespoon sea salt

Garlic Dill Pickles

12 ounces pickling cucumbers (2–3 cucumbers)

8 sprigs of dill

½ tablespoon whole peppercorns

½ tablespoon whole mustard seed

1 tablespoon sea salt

¾ cup distilled white vinegar

6 cloves garlic, chopped

1. For Classic Crunch, Tangy Garlic, and Garlic Dill Pickles: Slice the cucumbers as desired (into slices, spears, or halves) or even leave them whole.

2. Add all the ingredients to a 16-ounce glass jar and top off with water. Seal and place in the refrigerator for 4 to 6 hours before eating.

1. For Red-Hot Pickles: Slice the cucumbers as desired and set aside.

2. Place the vinegar and coconut crystals in a 16-ounce jar and stir until dissolved. Add in the remaining ingredients.

3. Add the cucumbers to the jar, top off with water, seal, and place in the refrigerator for 4 to 6 hours before eating.

Continue to store your pickles in the refrigerator for up to 1 year.

Each recipe makes 1 jar of pickles.

Red-Hot Pickles
12 ounces pickling cucumbers (2–3 cucumbers)
¾ cup distilled white vinegar
1 tablespoon coconut crystals or other dry sweetener of your choice
6 sprigs of fresh dill
½ tablespoon whole peppercorns
2 cloves garlic, chopped
1 teaspoon sea salt
1 tablespoon crushed red pepper flakes

Giardiniera

These pickled vegetables have just the right amount of briny saltiness and heat from chili peppers to make your taste buds happy. Any burger would be thrilled to have this beautiful condiment at its side!

For step 1

1 red bell pepper, diced

4 yellow chili peppers or
   banana peppers, diced

1 celery stalk, diced

1 carrot, diced

1 small onion, diced

½ cup cauliflower florets

½ cup salt

Water to cover

For step 2

2 cloves garlic, minced

1 tablespoon dried oregano

1 teaspoon red pepper flakes

½ teaspoon ground black
   pepper

¼ cup diced black or
   kalamata olives

¼ cup diced green olives

1 cup white vinegar

1 cup canola oil

1. Place the ingredients for step 1 in a large bowl. Stir well and then cover with plastic wrap and place in the refrigerator at least 8 hours. Drain and rinse the salty water from the vegetables.

2. Place the ingredients for step 2 into a small bowl and mix well. Pour the mixture over the vegetables and stir well. Be sure all the vegetables are coated with the vinegar and oil mixture. Cover and refrigerate for at least 2 days before consuming.

As with most pickled vegetables, Giardiniera gets better with time. Spoon it into a sealed container and it will keep in the refrigerator for 2 to 3 weeks.

Makes 2 cups.

Sweet and Tangy BBQ Sauce

A little sweet and just the right amount of tang. This barbecue sauce is perfect for burgers and baked beans, or as a tasty alternative to ketchup.

Place all the ingredients in a medium-sized saucepan and heat over low heat for 30 minutes, stirring occasionally. Use immediately or allow to cool completely before storing in an airtight container in the refrigerator for up to 4 weeks.

Makes 2¼ cups.

½ cup apple butter

¼ cup blackstrap molasses

7 ounces no-salt-added tomato paste

6 tablespoons apple cider vinegar

½ teaspoon garlic powder

½ teaspoon sea salt

Fun Fact: It's only been in recent years that blackstrap molasses has been finally getting the recognition it deserves as a "superfood." Just one tablespoon of molasses contains nearly 20 percent of the daily recommended value of iron, which provides energy, helps the body fight off infections, supports brain and muscle function, and improves immunity. It also contains over 17 percent of the daily recommended value of calcium. Molasses is an excellent source of the antioxidant manganese, which helps the body fight free-radical damage to cells and DNA.

A Hummus for All Occasions

Hummus is one of our favorite toppings for burgers, crackers, veggies, and sandwiches. It's so versatile and you can create so many tasty varieties. Here are three of our favorites.

Creamy Roasted Garlic Hummus

1¾ cups cooked garbanzo beans

1 whole head of garlic, roasted (for instructions, see Step 2 of the Sweet Roasted Garlic Mustard recipe, page 114)

1 tablespoon freshly squeezed lemon juice

2 tablespoons extra-virgin olive oil

1 teaspoon oregano

Marinated Artichoke Hummus

1¾ cups cooked garbanzo beans

1¾ cups cooked artichoke hearts

2 tablespoons white balsamic vinegar

3 tablespoons extra-virgin olive oil

2–3 cloves garlic, minced

2 tablespoons freshly squeezed lemon juice

1 teaspoon oregano

Sun-Dried Tomato Hummus

1¾ cups cooked garbanzo beans

2 tablespoons extra-virgin olive oil

2 cloves garlic, minced

3 tablespoons sun-dried tomatoes in oil

1 tablespoon parsley

2 tablespoons freshly squeezed lemon juice

For each recipe, place all of the ingredients in a blender or food processor and process until well blended. For a smoother variety, add in a small amount of additional olive oil until you've reached your desired consistency.

Store in an airtight container in the refrigerator for up to 2 weeks.

Each recipe makes approximately 2–3 cups of hummus.

Creamy Cashew Sauce

Nutritional yeast and smoked paprika give this sauce a smoky, cheesy flavor while the cashews create a smooth and rich flavor. It's an ideal dipping sauce for our Crispy Baked Taquitos (page 178), tortilla chips, and even raw veggies!

1. Process the cashews in a high-powered blender for about 20 seconds or until they are a sand-like consistency. Add the remaining ingredients and blend for 1 to 2 minutes more or until you have a smooth, creamy texture.

2. Transfer the mixture to a medium-sized saucepan and heat on medium low for about 10 minutes, stirring frequently.

3. Remove from heat and serve over Crispy Baked Taquitos, a baked potato, pasta, or your favorite bean or veggie burger.

Store in an airtight container in the refrigerator for up to 1 week.

Makes approximately 1½ cups.

- ½ cup unsalted raw or roasted cashews
- 1 red pepper, seeded
- ¾ cup vegetable broth
- ⅛ cup canola or other neutral-flavor oil
- ½ teaspoon sea salt
- ¼ cup nutritional yeast
- ¼ teaspoon garlic powder
- ½ teaspoon smoked paprika

Sweet Corn Ceviche

Fresh, sweet corn is the star of this recipe. This dish is a perfect addition to any meal and can also be used in quesadillas, salads, or mixed in with pasta.

2 ears fresh raw corn on the cob
Zest and juice of one lime
2 tablespoons high-quality extra-virgin olive oil
1 green onion, finely chopped
1 serrano chile, seeded and minced
¼ cup chopped fresh cilantro, parsley, or oregano
¼ teaspoon sea salt

1. Using a sharp knife, cut the corn kernels from the cobs and place them in a mixing bowl.

2. Add the lime zest and juice, olive oil, green onion, chile, and stir to coat.

3. Add the cilantro and sea salt and mix until thoroughly combined. Let sit for at least 30 minutes before serving so the flavors can blend.

Store in the refrigerator for up to 2 days.

Makes 2 cups.

Fun Fact: When it comes to cilantro, you either love it or hate it. Cilantro contains a natural chemical compound called an aldehyde. Aldehydes are also produced in the soap-making process and by some insects. For this reason, some people describe the flavor of cilantro as soapy or as similar to the scent of a stink bug. How we interpret the flavor of aldehydes is partly rooted in genetics. Two olfactory receptor genes have recently been discovered that link to our interpretation of cilantro as either soapy or herbal. If you find cilantro to have an unpleasant taste, try substituting it with either parsley or oregano.

Miso Dijonnaise

Creamy, tangy, and delicious, this topping can be ready in minutes and is perfect for just about any burger. It will put your regular mayo to shame!

¼ cup nondairy milk

1 teaspoon freshly squeezed lemon juice

1 teaspoon rice vinegar

½ cup canola oil

2 tablespoons white or yellow miso

1 tablespoon Dijon mustard

½ teaspoon sea salt

⅛ teaspoon ground white pepper

1. Place the milk, lemon juice, and vinegar in a small blender or food processor.

2. Let sit a minute, then add the remaining ingredients and blend until thick and smooth.

If desired, add more miso for a tangier flavor or to make a thicker dressing.

Store in an airtight container in the refrigerator for up to 10 days.

Makes 1 cup.

Ranch Dressing

Ranch dressing is easily one of the most popular condiments that we use. It's perfect for salads, veggies, sandwiches, burgers, and fries. Here is a quick and easy recipe that can be customized to your individual taste.

1. Place the vinegar and milk in a food processor or powerful blender and let sit for 5 minutes. Add the oil and process for about 15 seconds.

2. Add the remaining ingredients and pulse 3 or 4 times until thoroughly combined and somewhat thick (perfect as a dip). If you want a thinner dressing, add in a bit more milk until you've reached your desired consistency.

Store in an airtight container in the refrigerator for up to 2 weeks.

Makes 2 cups.

1 teaspoon apple cider vinegar
½ cup unsweetened plain soy milk
1 cup canola oil or other neutral-flavor oil of your choice (e.g., grapeseed, sunflower, or safflower)
2–3 cloves garlic or 1 teaspoon garlic powder
½ teaspoon onion powder
1–2 tablespoons finely chopped fresh parsley
1–2 tablespoons finely chopped fresh chives
Sea salt and black pepper to taste

Quick Tip: Use this recipe as a starting-off point to create your perfect ranch flavor. Add some dill or Dijon mustard for a fun twist.

Tangy Tartar Sauce

While this is the perfect condiment for our Happy Crabby Patty burgers (page 66), it's also great as a dip for veggies or an alternative to mayo on sandwiches.

¼ cup nondairy milk

1 teaspoon freshly squeezed lemon juice

½ cup canola oil

3 tablespoons no-salt-added tomato paste

2–3 tablespoons minced dill pickles

1 teaspoon dry mustard

1 teaspoon capers (about 5–6 berries)

½ teaspoon Old Bay Seasoning

hot sauce to taste

1. Combine the milk and lemon juice in a food processor (do not stir) and let it sit for a minute, allowing the liquids to slightly thicken.

2. Add the remaining ingredients and process until thick and smooth.

Store in an airtight container in the fridge for 7 to 10 days.

Makes 1 cup.

Marinated Purple Cabbage

Don't you just love recipes that you can use more than once? This marinated cabbage is awesome for adding to salads, stir-fries, and pasta dishes. It can also garnish your favorite sandwich or burger. A simple recipe with so many uses!

1. In a large bowl, mix together the vinegar, coconut nectar, sea salt, and oil. Add in the cabbage and mix well to coat.

2. Cover the bowl with a lid and place in the fridge for 24 to 48 hours, turning the cabbage over every 6 to 8 hours The cabbage will turn a reddish purple color once it's done marinating. To serve, drain the cabbage and discard the liquid.

Store in the refrigerator for up to 3 weeks.

Makes approximately 3 cups.

1½ cups red wine vinegar

1½ tablespoons coconut nectar, honey, or brown rice syrup

½ tablespoon sea salt

Drizzle of extra-virgin olive oil

3 cups thinly shredded purple cabbage

Fun Fact: Cabbage is a rich source of vitamin C, fiber, iron, calcium, and potassium. The odor that it emits comes from its sulphur content, which helps the body to resist bacteria and protects the protoplasm of the cells. Cabbage is said to help promote glossy hair.

Quick and Easy Pickled Red Onion

Onions are a natural burger topping that can be served in many different ways, from raw to fried. These pickled onions are easy to make and delicious on burgers.

1 cup water

½ cup red wine vinegar

2 teaspoons sea salt

4 whole black peppercorns

1 red onion, thinly sliced

1. Place the water, vinegar, salt, and peppercorns into a small nonreactive saucepan. Bring to a boil and remove from the heat.

2. Add the onion and stir well. Let cool, stirring occasionally. Drain and serve.

Store in an airtight container in the refrigerator for 3 to 4 weeks.

Makes approximately 1 cup.

Rockin' Creamy Almond Sauce

If you were to take a peek in our fridge, you would always find a batch of this sauce on hand. We use it as a condiment for burgers, a dressing for salads, a dip for veggies, french fries, and chips, a topping for a baked potato, or even a spread for a sandwich or wrap. The options are endless and all delicious!

Place all the ingredients in a food processor or blender and process until smooth and creamy. The sauce will thicken as it sits. For a thinner sauce, add in a bit more water or oil until you reach the desired consistency.

Store in an airtight container in the refrigerator for up to 3 weeks.

Makes 1½ cups.

Quick Tip: For a rockin' accompaniment to salads, soups, and pasta dishes, slice a baguette in half and spread a layer of Rockin' Creamy Almond Sauce on top. Top with nondairy cheese of your choice and bake in a preheated oven at 350°F for 5 to 10 minutes or until the cheese is melted and golden brown.

- ¾ cup almonds (raw or roasted both provide good flavor)
- ¼ cup shelled hemp seeds
- ¼ cup plus 2 tablespoons freshly squeezed lemon juice
- ¼ cup plus 2 tablespoons canola oil or other neutral-flavor oil
- 1 clove garlic, minced
- 2 tablespoons nutritional yeast
- 3 tablespoons soy sauce or tamari (gluten-free if needed)
- ½ teaspoon smoked paprika
- ½ teaspoon black pepper
- ½ teaspoon cumin
- ¼ teaspoon mustard powder
- ⅛ teaspoon chili powder
- Pinch of sea salt
- ¼ cup plus 2 tablespoons water

Avocado Relish

Avocado Relish is so creamy and full of fresh flavor that it makes a great topping on many different burgers. Make extra and serve it with chips on the side to round out your meal.

2 ripe Hass avocados, peeled, pitted, and diced

4 tablespoons finely diced red onion

1 Fresno chili pepper, seeded and finely diced

2 tablespoons freshly squeezed lemon juice

2 tablespoons olive oil

2 teaspoons maple syrup

Sea salt and black pepper to taste

2 tablespoons finely chopped parsley

Combine all of the ingredients in a bowl. Let sit 5 to 10 minutes before serving.

Store in an airtight container in the refrigerator for 2 to 3 days.

Makes approximately 1½ cups.

Fun Fact: During the fat-free diet craze in the '90s, avocados got a bad rap due to their higher fat content. While avocados do have a high fat content for a fruit, they are still considered to be one of the healthiest foods on the planet as they contain more than 25 essential nutrients, including vitamins A, B, C, E, and K, copper, iron, phosphorus, magnesium, and potassium. Avocados also contain fiber, protein, and several beneficial phytochemicals such as beta-sitosterol, glutathione, and lutein.

Cashew Parmesan

This simple recipe is a beloved staple in our pantry. It's excellent for adding to pasta, potatoes, salads, and soups. Make a double or triple batch and store in the refrigerator for up to 6 months, or up to a year in the freezer.

½ **cup toasted cashews**
¼ **cup nutritional yeast**
1 teaspoon coarse sea salt

Place the cashews in a food processor and process until finely ground. Add the nutritional yeast and salt. Pulse once or twice to mix.

Makes approximately ½ cup.

Coconut "Bacon" Bites

If you look in our pantry on any given day, you will likely find a stash of Coconut "Bacon" Bites. We love sprinkling them on salads, burgers, and sandwiches. Don't be surprised if you find yourself sneaking a handful to snack on throughout the day—they are that good!

1. Preheat the oven to 325°F.

2. In a medium-sized mixing bowl, whisk together the first four ingredients. Add the coconut flakes and stir well until evenly coated.

3. Transfer the coconut flakes to a large glass baking dish or parchment-lined baking sheet. Spread the coconut flakes out in an even single layer and spinkle with sea salt if desired.

4. Bake in the oven for 20 to 25 minutes or until nicely browned and caramelized, stirring every 5 minutes.

5. Let cool for 5 minutes before serving.

Store in an airtight container in the pantry for 1 to 2 weeks.

Makes 3½ cups.

2½ tablespoons soy sauce or tamari

1 tablespoon liquid smoke

1 tablespoon maple syrup

1 teaspoon smoked paprika

3½ cups large flaked coconut

Sea salt (optional)

Quick Tip: For a fun take on the traditional BLT, spread a layer of Miso Dijonnaise (page 124) or Rockin' Creamy Almond Sauce (page 129) on a flour tortilla, sprinkle a handful of Coconut "Bacon" Bites, top with fresh lettuce and sliced tomato, roll up, and enjoy!

SIDES AND SALADS

Sweet Potato Beer Fries

These fries are so yummy and delicious that you might never eat sweet potatoes any other way again. They are the perfect side to your favorite burger.

3 pounds sweet potatoes, scrubbed

1 bottle organic beer of your choice

3 tablespoons olive oil

2–3 cloves garlic, minced

½ teaspoon oregano

1 teaspoon coarse sea salt

Freshly ground black pepper to taste

1. Preheat the oven to 425°F. Line a baking sheet with parchment paper or nonstick foil and set aside.

2. Cut the potatoes into ¼-inch-thick pieces with the skins left on. Place the potatoes in a large bowl, add the bottle of beer, and let the potatoes soak for 15 to 30 minutes.

3. Drain the beer and toss the potatoes with olive oil, garlic, oregano, salt, and pepper until well coated.

4. Spread the fries on the prepared baking sheet in a single layer. Bake for 45 minutes to 1 hour, tossing 3 to 4 times (the length of time will depend on how done you like them and how thick they are cut). Remove the fries and serve immediately.

Makes 4–6 servings.

Fun Fact: A 7-ounce (1-cup) serving of sweet potatoes contains 65 percent of the minimum daily amount of vitamin C. Sweet potatoes are also high in calcium, folate, potassium, beta-carotene, and vitamin A. In fact, 700 percent of the recommended daily allowance of vitamin A is met with just one serving of this super tuber!

Smoky Ranch Potato Salad

This creamy potato salad is made with smoked paprika that creates a hint of bacon-like flavor. So simple yet so scrumptious!

1. Place the potatoes and salt in a large pot. Add water to cover. Bring to a boil and reduce heat to a simmer. Cook, uncovered, until just tender when pierced with a knife, approximately 12 to 15 minutes.

2. Drain the water and set aside until the potatoes are cool enough to handle. Once cooled, cut into bite-sized pieces.

3. In a small bowl whisk together the ranch dressing, paprika, coconut aminos, mustard, and maple sugar.

4. Add any additional veggies if desired and then fold the dressing gently onto the potatoes, taking care not to mash them. Cover and refrigerate for 2 to 3 hours to allow the flavors to meld. Serve chilled.

Store in an airtight container in the refrigerator for 2 to 3 days.

Makes approximately 6 cups.

8 good-sized red skin potatoes, quartered
½ teaspoon sea salt
1 cup Ranch Dressing (page 125)
2 teaspoons smoked paprika
1 teaspoon coconut aminos or tamari (gluten-free if needed)
1 teaspoon dry mustard
1 teaspoon maple sugar
¼ cup diced green or red pepper (optional)
½ cup frozen peas, thawed (optional)
1 stalk celery, diced (optional)
2 red radishes, diced (optional)

Fun Fact: Red potatoes contain high levels of antioxidants called anthocyanins, which help to prevent ulcers, diabetes, and heart disease. The red potato contains five times the level of antioxidants of the russet potato. If red potatoes are not available, opt instead for blue or purple potatoes, as these are the most nutritious varieties.

Peanutty Brussels Slaw

This slaw made with Brussels sprouts is light and delicious and tossed with one of the most flavorful dressings ever to coat a cruciferous vegetable.

1 cup thinly sliced Brussels
    sprouts
2 cups thinly sliced Napa
    cabbage
1 carrot, shredded
2 tablespoons no-salt-added
    peanut butter
¼ cup olive oil
2 tablespoons apple cider
    vinegar
1 tablespoon coconut nectar,
    honey, or brown rice syrup
Sea salt to taste
2 tablespoons raw peanuts,
    coarsely chopped

1. Toss together the Brussels sprouts, cabbage, and carrot in a large bowl.

2. In a small bowl, whisk together the peanut butter, oil, vinegar, coconut nectar, and sea salt until smooth. Set the mixture aside.

3. Toast the peanuts in a dry skillet over medium heat for 3 to 4 minutes or until just turning brown.

4. Pour the peanut butter mixture over the vegetables and toss to coat. Garnish with the toasted peanuts and serve.

If the dressing and salad are stored separately, they will keep in the refrigerator for 3 to 4 days.

Makes 4 servings.

Fun Fact: Many people say they dislike Brussels sprouts because of their sulfurous odor, but the sprouts only omit the odor when overcooked. Brussels sprouts are an excellent source of vitamin A, vitamin C (way more than an orange, by the way), and vitamin K, as well as beta-carotene, folic acid, iron, magnesium, and fiber. They're also high in selenium, which is associated with reduced risks of certain cancers. Look for sprouts that are still on the stalk; they not only last longer but are usually cheaper.

Tangy Three-Bean Salad

Refreshing and tangy, this simple salad bursts with flavor.

1. In a large bowl, mix together the beans, cucumber, onion, and parsley. In a separate small bowl, whisk together the vinegar, coconut nectar, olive oil, salt, garlic, and mustard. Add the dressing to the beans and gently stir to coat.

2. Refrigerate the salad for several hours to allow the beans to soak up the flavor of the dressing. Serve chilled or at room temperature.

Store in an airtight container in the refrigerator for up to 1 week.

Makes approximately 8 cups.

Fun Fact: *Did you know that canned beans are even higher in antioxidants than home-cooked beans? The heat of the canning process enhances the nutritional content of the beans. If you do cook your own beans, steam or pressure-cook them to retain their antioxidant value. If you don't have a pressure cooker and opt to simmer the beans instead, use the cooking water in your recipe or let the beans soak in the cooking water for an hour after they are done so they can reabsorb some of the nutrients.*

1¾ cups cooked cannellini beans

1¾ cups cooked kidney beans

1¾ cups cooked garbanzo beans

1 cucumber, seeded and finely diced

½ red onion, finely minced

¾ cup fresh parsley, finely chopped

⅓ cup apple cider vinegar

1 tablespoon coconut nectar, honey, or brown rice syrup

2½ tablespoons extra-virgin olive oil

1½ teaspoons sea salt

2–3 cloves garlic, minced

1 tablespoon Dijon mustard

Crispy Sesame Green Bean Fries

These "fries" are so delicious and addictive that you might never eat a regular french fry again. Even the pickiest of eaters will be asking for more.

2 handfuls of fresh green beans (about 50 beans), ends trimmed

½ cup lite coconut milk

1 tablespoon sesame oil (toasted sesame oil adds a great flavor too)

¾ cup Homemade Bread Crumbs (page 108)

3 tablespoons sesame seeds

¼ cup whole grain flour (whole wheat, spelt, brown rice, or even millet will work)

1. Preheat the oven to 425°F. Line a baking sheet with parchment paper or nonstick foil and set aside. Fill a large bowl with ice water and set aside.

2. Bring a pot of water to a boil over high heat. Add the green beans and cook until tender, about 5 minutes. Remove the beans with a slotted spoon and transfer to the ice water to stop the cooking. Let cool in the water, then drain and pat dry.

3. In a small bowl, whisk together the coconut milk and sesame oil. Set aside. In a medium bowl, combine the bread crumbs and sesame seeds. Set aside. In a large bowl, combine the green beans and flour. Gently mix together until the green beans are well coated.

4. Dip each floured green bean in the coconut milk mixture and then dredge through the bread crumbs. Place on the baking sheet and repeat with the remaining green beans.

5. Bake for 20 to 25 minutes or until browned and crisp, flipping the fries over once halfway through cooking. Remove from the oven and serve immediately.

Makes 4 servings.

Quick Tip: Raw fresh green beans, also called snap beans or French beans, should be tender, long, and stiff, but flexible and able to make a snapping sound when broken. Try to avoid limp or overly matured beans with tough skin. To store, place them in a perforated plastic bag and keep inside the refrigerator set at high relative humidity. They keep well for up to a week.

Macaroni Salad

What cookout or potluck would be complete without macaroni salad? This recipe is inspired by the old classic but our Miso Dijonnaise gives it a fun and tasty new twist.

12 ounces elbow macaroni of your choice

1 cup peas (thaw if frozen)

1 large carrot, finely diced

¼ cup finely diced red onion

Chopped radish, bell pepper, celery, tomato, or olives (optional)

1 cup Miso Dijonnaise (page 124)

½ teaspoon Italian seasoning

½ teaspoon sea salt or to taste

1. Cook the pasta according to the directions on the package. Drain and rinse with cold water.

2. Transfer the pasta to a large bowl and add in the peas, carrot, and red onion. Add in any of the optional vegetables if desired. Stir well and set aside.

3. In a small bowl, gently mix together the Miso Dijonnaise, Italian seasoning, and sea salt. Add the sauce to the pasta and stir well until thoroughly combined.

4. Place in the refrigerator for 30 minutes before serving.

Makes 8 cups.

Chuckwagon Beans

Here's an old classic that has been updated Naked Kitchen–style.

1. Preheat the oven to 350°F.

2. Heat the oil in a large skillet over medium-high heat. Add the mushrooms, onion, smoked paprika, salt, and pepper and sauté until the vegetables are tender, about 5 minutes.

3. Add the chili sauce, ketchup, coconut crystals, vinegar, and mustard. Stir to combine and bring to a simmer. Simmer for 1 to 2 minutes and remove from heat.

4. In a large casserole dish (at least 2-quart size), combine all the beans and the mushroom-and-onion sauce.

5. Bake uncovered for 1 hour. Serve with your favorite burger and enjoy!

Store in an airtight container in the refrigerator for 4 to 5 days.

Makes 8 cups.

- 2 tablespoons olive oil
- 8 ounces cremini mushrooms, diced
- 1 onion, diced
- 1 teaspoon smoked paprika
- 1 teaspoon sea salt
- ½ teaspoon black pepper
- ½ cup Sweet Heat Chili Sauce (page 111)
- ½ cup ketchup
- ½ cup coconut crystals or other dry sweetener of your choice
- 3 tablespoons white vinegar
- 1 teaspoon dry mustard
- 1¾ cups cooked navy or great northern beans
- 1¾ cups cut green beans
- 1¾ cups cut yellow or wax beans
- 1¾ cups kidney beans
- 1¾ cups lima or fava beans

Broccoli Salad

We've made many broccoli salads over the years, but this one is hands-down the best we've ever had. You get all the crunch and cheesy bacon flavor of the original without the guilt and unhealthy ingredients. This salad is the perfect side to any meal.

1. Place the first ten ingredients in a blender (or a powerful food processor) and process until smooth. Set aside.

2. In a large bowl, combine the broccoli, red onion, almonds, and raisins (if using) and toss to combine. Add the desired amount of dressing and mix thoroughly until well coated.

3. Sprinkle with sunflower seeds and enjoy.

Store in an airtight container in the refrigerator for 2 to 3 days.

Makes 9 cups.

Fun Fact: Broccoli has been around for more than two thousand years and was a favorite vegetable of the Romans. It's an excellent source of vitamins A and C, potassium, iron, and fiber and has as much calcium per ounce as milk. When purchasing broccoli, choose bunches that are dark green with very firm stalks. Good color indicates high nutrient value. Florets that are dark green, purplish, or bluish green contain more beta-carotene and vitamin C than paler or yellowing ones. Avoid broccoli with open, flowering, discolored, or water-soaked bud clusters and tough, woody stems.

½ cup shelled hemp seeds

2 teaspoons freshly squeezed lemon juice

1 clove garlic, minced

1 tablespoon chickpea miso or sweet white miso

¼ cup water

1 tablespoon coconut nectar, honey, or brown rice syrup

½ teaspoon sea salt

4 tablespoons nutritional yeast

½ cup extra-virgin olive oil

¼ teaspoon smoked paprika

8 cups broccoli, roughly chopped into small pieces

½ small red onion, diced

¾ cup Tastes Like Bacon Almonds (see next recipe), roughly chopped

½ cup raisins (optional)

Sunflower seeds to garnish

Tastes Like Bacon Almonds

Maple sugar and smoked paprika combine to give these ordinary almonds a tasty kick of bacon-like flavors. They are excellent on their own as a yummy treat or added to salads and other dishes.

1 teaspoon dry mustard

2 teaspoons fine sea salt

2 teaspoons maple sugar

3 teaspoons smoked paprika, divided

2 teaspoons peanut oil

1 cup raw almonds

1 teaspoon coconut aminos or tamari (gluten-free if needed)

1. Preheat the oven to 250°F. Line a baking sheet with parchment paper and set aside.

2. In a small bowl combine the dry mustard, sea salt, maple sugar, and 1 teaspoon of the paprika. Set aside.

3. Heat the oil in a skillet over medium heat. Add the remaining 2 teaspoons of the paprika and stir well. Add the almonds and stir to coat. Cook, stirring frequently, until toasted, about 4 to 5 minutes.

4. Add the coconut aminos and cook another few seconds until the liquid is absorbed. Sprinkle the dry spice mixture evenly over the almonds and toss to coat. Spread the almonds over the baking sheet in a single layer and bake for 20 minutes, stirring occasionally.

Store in a cool, dry place for up to 4 weeks.

Makes 1 cup.

Crunchy Apple and Cabbage Salad

This side salad delivers the ideal combination of crunch and flavor, and will complement just about any burger you serve it with.

1. In a large bowl, combine the cabbage, apple, and cherries.

2. In a small bowl, whisk together the oil, vinegar, maple syrup, mustard, coriander, and salt until smooth.

3. Just before serving, toss the dressing with the cabbage mixture, and serve garnished with the toasted pecans.

If stored separately, the dressing and salad will keep in the refrigerator for up to 4 days.

Makes 6–8 cups.

Fun Fact: *Over the years, apples have been crossbred to be larger, smoother skinned, shinier, and sweeter. As as result, some apples today, such as Ginger Gold, have lost so many of their phytonutrients that they fail even to register on the scale. Varieties such as Braeburn, Cortland, Discovery, Gala, Granny Smith, Honey Crisp, Idared, McIntosh, Ozark Gold, and Red Delicious have the most phytonutrients. Just make sure you eat the skins, as an unpeeled apple can contain 50 percent more phytonutrients than a peeled apple. Also note that apples last up to ten times longer stored in the refrigerator than at room temperature.*

1 small head savoy cabbage (green or Napa cabbage will also work), thinly sliced
1 medium apple, julienned
¼ cup dried unsweetened cherries
¼ cup canola or other neutral-flavor oil
¼ cup red wine vinegar
3 tablespoons maple syrup
2 tablespoons Dijon mustard
1 teaspoon ground coriander
¼ teaspoon sea salt
¼ cup chopped pecans, toasted

Tropical Fruit Skewers with Caramel Sauce

Grilling fruit really enhances its flavor, and when you add this caramel sauce, it's over the top. A delightful dessert for those warm summer nights!

½ cup coconut crystals or other dry sweetener of your choice

2 tablespoons water

2 tablespoons coconut milk

2 tablespoons coconut butter

2 teaspoons freshly squeezed lime juice

Pinch of sea salt

1 cup pineapple cubes

1 cup mango cubes

1 cup papaya cubes

1 cup banana chunks (optional)

1. Place the coconut crystals and water in a small saucepan over medium-high heat and bring to a boil, stirring until dissolved. Continue to cook until the liquid starts to get thick around the edges of the pan. This will only take about 1 minute, so be careful not to overcook and burn the sugar.

2. Carefully add the coconut milk and coconut butter (it will bubble up when added) and continue to cook, stirring constantly until thickened enough to coat the back of the spoon.

3. Add the lime juice and salt. Stir and set aside.

4. Thread the fruit chunks onto skewers. Heat your grill or grill pan over high heat. Grill the fruit until it's warmed through and shows nice grill marks, about 1 to 2 minutes on each side.

5. Place the fruit skewers on a platter and drizzle with the caramel sauce.

Makes 6–8 skewers.

Quick Tip: Have you ever been told never to put bananas in the refrigerator? While you wouldn't want to put unripe bananas in the refrigerator, you can allow them to fully ripen at room temperature and then store them in the refrigerator. They will keep a few days longer than if you kept them at room temperature. The skin will turn brown but the flesh will stay edible.

Spicy Sesame Noodle Salad

We love serving pasta in the form of noodle salads, and this is one of the best. Enjoy a bowl for lunch on a hot summer day, or make it your go-to potluck dish—just be prepared to leave with an empty bowl!

1. Prepare the noodles according to the directions on the package. After cooking, drain and rinse with cold water. Set aside.

2. In a large bowl, whisk together the soy sauce, ginger, orange juice, and hot pepper sesame oil. Add in the noodles, carrot, cucumber, snow peas, and green onion. Toss until everything is well coated.

3. Place the noodle salad in the fridge for at least 15 minutes or until well chilled. Serve with crushed peanuts as an optional garnish.

Store in an airtight container in the refrigerator for 4 to 5 days.

Makes 6–8 servings.

Quick Tip: Spring roll wrappers (aka rice paper wraps) can transform this recipe into a fun, dippable finger food. Place a spring roll wrapper in a bowl of water for 6 to 8 seconds. Remove the wrapper and place on a solid surface (the wrapper should still be somewhat stiff; it will soften as it absorbs the water). Place a small amount of noodles down the center of the wrapper. Top with a few carrots, cucumbers, snow peas, and green onion. Sprinkle with some crushed peanuts and then fold the wrapper in half and continue to roll up until completely sealed. Add the remaining ingredients to a small bowl and mix the dipping sauce well. Serve the spring rolls with a side of dipping sauce and enjoy!

12 ounces noodles of your choice

¾ cup plus 2 tablespoons soy sauce or tamari (gluten-free if needed)

3½ teaspoons minced ginger

¾ cup freshly squeezed orange juice

6–8 tablespoons hot pepper sesame oil (adjust to your desired heat level)

¾ cup grated or julienned carrot

¾ cup diced cucumber

½ cup thinly sliced snow peas, ends removed

¼ cup thinly sliced green onion

Crushed peanuts (optional garnish)

Crunchy Baked Onion Rings

While we love a good french fry, onion rings are our favorite burger side dish. There is nothing like a crispy, crunchy, flavorful onion ring. Enjoy!

2 yellow or sweet onions

1 cup nondairy milk

1 teaspoon apple cider vinegar

Heaping ½ cup whole-wheat flour

2 cups Homemade Bread Crumbs (page 108)

¼ cup Chickenless Bouillon Mix (page 20)

Olive oil for spraying (optional)

1. Preheat the oven to 400°F. Line a baking sheet with nonstick foil or parchment paper and set aside.

2. Slice the onions width-wise into your desired thickness and then break them apart into rings.

3. Combine the milk and vinegar in a bowl and let sit for about 5 minutes. Add the flour and mix well.

4. In a separate bowl (wide enough for dipping the onion rings), mix together the bread crumbs and bouillon mix well.

5. Dip each onion ring into the wet flour mixture and then into bread crumb mixture. Make sure each onion ring is evenly coated and then place on the prepared baking sheet.

6. Lightly spray your onion rings with olive oil if desired. Bake for 8 to 10 minutes, flip the onion rings over, and then bake for 8 to 12 minutes more or until golden brown. Serve hot out of the oven.

Makes 4–6 servings.

Quick Tip: Our Homemade Bread Crumbs are so full of flavor that no store-bought seasoned bread crumbs will come close in comparison. If you do decide to purchase store-bought bread crumbs, you will need to add seasoning in order to avoid a bland onion ring (this also works for other recipes that require our Homemade Bread Crumbs). Take 1 cup unseasoned store-bought bread crumbs and add 5 to 6 tablespoons nutritional yeast, ½ to 1 tablespoon garlic salt, ¼ to ½ tablespoon onion powder, and ½ tablespoon oregano. Mix well, give it a taste, and add more seasoning if desired.

Oriental Carrot Slaw

These crisp, crunchy vegetables are tossed in a smooth and creamy dressing with an oriental flair. This is not your average slaw! It's fantastic when paired with our Asian Quinoa Burger (page 26), Zucchini Almond Burger (page 50), or Spoon Burger (page 74).

1. Place the carrots, bok choy, and fennel in a large serving bowl. Set aside

2. In a blender or food processor, combine the milk and lemon juice. Let sit for 1 to 2 minutes, then add the oil and salt. Blend or process until thick and creamy.

3. Add the coconut nectar, vinegar, mustard, and sesame oil. Pulse to combine.

4. Pour the desired amount of dressing over the vegetables. Toss to coat. Let sit for about 15 minutes before serving.

Store in an airtight container in the refrigerator for up to 2 days.

Makes 4–5 cups.

- 4 cups shredded carrots
- 1 bunch bok choy, cut into thin strips
- 1 fennel bulb, cut into thin strips
- ¼ cup unsweetened soy milk
- 1 teaspoon freshly squeezed lemon juice
- ½ cup canola or other neutral-flavor oil
- ¼ teaspoon sea salt
- 3 tablespoons coconut nectar, honey, or brown rice syrup
- 4 tablespoons rice wine vinegar
- 2 teaspoons Dijon mustard
- ½ teaspoon toasted sesame oil

Fun Fact: Like all members of the cruciferous vegetable family, bok choy has unique sulfur-containing compounds that may reduce the risk of breast, prostate, lung, and digestive tract cancers. These substances may help the body to eliminate carcinogens, prevent cells from turning cancerous, or alter metabolism to stop the development of hormone-sensitive cancers. One cup of shredded bok choy has 34 percent of the recommended daily value of vitamin C and more than a full day's intake of vitamin A.

Wasabi Pea and Peanut Salad

Pea and peanut salad is a classic, but for those who crave something a little bit bolder, this recipe with a kick of wasabi is just the thing.

¼ cup nondairy milk, chilled

1 teaspoon freshly squeezed lemon juice

½ cup canola or other neutral-flavor oil

½ teaspoon sea salt

2 tablespoons rice vinegar

2 teaspoons coconut nectar, honey, or brown rice syrup

2 teaspoons wasabi powder or to taste

1 teaspoon sesame oil

3 cups frozen green peas, thawed and drained

1 cup peanuts

¼ cup diced red onion

1 rib celery, diced

1. Combine the milk and lemon juice in a blender or food processor (do not stir) and let sit for 1 to 2 minutes, allowing the liquids to thicken.

2. Add the oil and blend until thickened. Add the salt, vinegar, coconut nectar, wasabi powder, and sesame oil and blend until the dressing is just mixed.

3. Place the peas, peanuts, onion, and celery in a serving bowl. Add the dressing and stir to combine.

Store in an airtight container in the refrigerator for up to 2 days.

Makes 4 cups.

Fun Fact: When your mom told you to eat your peas, she knew what she was talking about. Green peas have twice the protein of most vegetables and are rich in iron and vitamin C. Green peas also help to build strong bones. Just one cup of peas contains 44 percent of your daily recommended value of vitamin K, which helps to anchor calcium inside the bones. Also, its B vitamins help to prevent osteoporosis.

Fava Beans with Peppers and Tomatoes

This Mediterranean medley hits all the right notes of sweet, salty, tangy, savory, and delicious. A perfect topping for Roasted Eggplant Patties, Sun-Dried Tomato and Pepper Sausages, a green salad, or all on its own.

1. Heat the oil in a large skillet over medium-high heat. Add the onion, carrot, red pepper, and salt and sauté for 4 to 5 minutes or until the vegetables are tender.

2. Add the tomatoes, garlic, capers, and celery leaves and cook for another 1 to 2 minutes.

3. Stir in the lemon zest, oregano, and pepper. Then add the beans and olives and cook until heated through, about 2 to 3 minutes. Garnish with additional chopped celery leaves if desired.

Store in an airtight container in the refrigerator for 3 to 4 days.

Makes 3 cups.

Fun Fact: *Fava beans are dense with nutrition. Also known as broad beans, fava beans have no saturated fat or cholesterol and contain a high concentration of thiamin, vitamin K, vitamin B-6, potassium, copper, selenium, zinc, and magnesium. They are also an inexpensive source of lean protein. A serving of cooked or fresh fava beans can significantly increase your intake of folate, iron, manganese, and dietary fiber—all nutrients that can benefit your health in a variety of ways.*

2 tablespoons extra-virgin olive oil

1 cup diced yellow onion

½ cup diced carrot

½ cup diced red pepper

½ teaspoon sea salt, divided

½ cup diced tomatoes

2 cloves garlic, minced

1 teaspoon capers, chopped

2 tablespoons minced celery leaves (use the tender leaves at the center of the bunch)

1 tablespoon lemon zest

1 teaspoon oregano

½–1 teaspoon ground black pepper according to taste

1¾ cups cooked fava beans

¼ cup pitted and sliced kalamata olives

Massaged Kale Salad

Who doesn't like a good massage? Well, kale is no exception! Kale is a somewhat tough green, but when you massage the leaves it helps to break down the fibers, resulting in a softer texture and a less bitter taste. You'll never want to eat kale any other way.

⅓ cup soy sauce or tamari (gluten-free if needed)

¼ cup extra-virgin olive oil

1 tablespoon Dijon mustard

½ tablespoon freshly squeezed lemon juice

1 tablespoon apple cider vinegar

1–2 cloves garlic, minced

5–6 cups chopped kale, stems removed

1 cup diced cucumbers

1 cup diced carrots

¼ cup finely diced red onion

½ cup toasted sliced almonds

1. In a large bowl, mix together the soy sauce, olive oil, mustard, lemon juice, vinegar, and garlic. Stir well until the dressing is blended.

2. Add the kale and, using your hands, gently massage the dressing into the kale. As you work the dressing into the leaves, you should notice them turning a bright green color.

3. Place the remaining ingredients in the bowl and toss until everything is well coated. Serve immediately.

Store in an airtight container in the refrigerator for up to 3 days.

Makes 4–6 servings.

Fun Fact: Carrots have long been known to be good for the eyes, but that's not all they are good for. Carrots contains high amounts of vitamin A and other antioxidants that protect the skin from sun damage and prevent premature wrinkling, acne, dry skin, pigmentation, blemishes, and uneven skin tone. While eating carrots will help to keep your skin looking beautiful, you can also use them to make an inexpensive facial mask that will leave your skin glowing. Just mix grated carrot with a bit of honey and spread evenly on your face. Let sit for 2 to 3 minutes and then wash off with warm water.

Cornmeal-Crusted Zucchini Bites

This recipe is adapted from an old family recipe. These little bites of zucchini are crispy on the outside while remaining soft and creamy on the inside.

1. Mix together the first 6 ingredients. Spread the mixture on a plate or other flat dish.

2. Place the milk in a bowl and add the lemon juice and hot sauce. Stir and then let sit for 2 to 3 minutes.

3. Heat 2 tablespoons of the oil in a large nonstick skillet over medium heat. Meanwhile, place half of the zucchini slices in the milk mixture, making sure all of them are coated. Transfer the zucchini to the plate with the cornmeal mixture, laying them in a single layer. Flip the slices over to coat the other sides, and then place in the skillet.

4. Fry the zucchini for 4 to 5 minutes on each side or until brown and crispy on the outside and tender on the inside. Repeat with the remaining zucchini and serve.

Makes 2 servings.

½ cup cornmeal

¼ cup whole-wheat flour

1 teaspoon sea salt

1 teaspoon basil

¼ teaspoon black pepper

½ teaspoon garlic granules

¼ cup unsweetened soy milk
   (or other non-dairy milk for
   a soy-free option)

1 teaspoon freshly squeezed
   lemon juice

1 teaspoon (or to taste) hot
   sauce of your choice

4 tablespoons canola oil,
   divided

4 small zucchini, sliced into
   ¼-inch-thick rounds

Fun Fact: If you're starting to feel a little stiff in the joints, try adding more zucchini to your diet. Vitamins C and A not only serve the body as powerful antioxidants, but also as effective anti-inflammatory agents. Along with the copper found in zucchini, these vitamins deter the development of many hyper–inflammatory disorders, including asthma, osteoarthritis, and rheumatoid arthritis.

Summary Harvest Salad

Each year, our garden rewards us with loads of cherry tomatoes, cucumbers, corn, and other delicious vegetables and herbs. This salad is a celebration of summer's bounty.

½ cup extra-virgin olive oil

⅓ cup freshly squeezed lime juice

1 teaspoon grated lime zest

½ cup packed cilantro leaves

1 jalapeno pepper, stemmed and roughly chopped

Sea salt to taste

1½ cups cooked grains of your choice (e.g., brown rice, millet, quinoa, barley)

About 2 cups grilled corn, fresh off the cob (2–3 grilled ears of corn)

1 cup cherry or grape tomatoes, halved

1 cup diced cucumber

6 ounces salad greens of your choice

Heaping ¼ cup thinly sliced red onion

Sesame seeds (optional garnish)

1. Place the first 6 ingredients in a blender and process until smooth. Set the dressing aside.

2. In a large salad bowl, layer the grains, corn, tomatoes, cucumbers, salad greens, and onion. Drizzle the dressing over the top and garnish with sesame seeds if desired.

Makes 4–6 servings.

Fun Fact: *We've all heard the saying that milk does a body good, but apparently sesame seeds do a much better job! Whole sesame seeds contain about 88 mg of calcium per tablespoon of seeds. Just a quarter cup of natural sesame seeds provides more calcium than a whole cup of milk. A quarter cup of raw natural sesame seeds has 351 mg of calcium while one cup of nonfat milk has 316.3 mg, and one cup of whole milk has only 291 mg of calcium.*

BEYOND BURGERS

Potato Breakfast Hash

We will often make burgers during the week just so that we'll have leftovers that we can use to whip up this simple breakfast hash. It's one of our family's favorite breakfast meals, and sometimes you'll find us enjoying it for dinner, too!

2 large Yukon Gold potatoes, peeled or unpeeled

2 tablespoons olive oil or other neutral-flavor oil

½ cup diced red or yellow onion

½ medium red pepper, seeded and diced

1 teaspoon sea salt

Black pepper to taste

1 cup corn (thaw if frozen)

2 good-sized bean or vegetable burgers, crumbled (Zesty Bean Burger, Spicy Chili Burger, Buffalo Black Bean Burger, or Hearty Mushroom Burger all work great); or 2–3 Roasted Garlic Hummus Dogs, diced (page 198)

Finely diced chives (optional garnish)

1. Place the potatoes in a large pot and cover entirely with water. Bring to a boil and cook until the potatoes are fork tender. Remove them from water and let cool for 5 to 10 minutes. Place the potatoes on a cutting board and dice them into 1-inch pieces.

2. In a large skillet, heat the oil over medium heat. Add the onion and pepper to the skillet and sauté until the onions start to brown.

3. Add the potatoes to your skillet, stir well, then let them cook for about 5 minutes untouched. Season the potatoes with salt and pepper and use a spatula to flip them over. Continue to let the potatoes cook until they are golden brown and crispy.

4. Add in the corn and the crumbled burgers and stir well. Continue to cook for 2 minutes more. Remove from heat and serve immediately. Garnish with chives if desired.

Store in an airtight container in the refrigerator for up to 2 days.

Makes 4 servings.

Quick Tip: This dish is delicious served over a crusty piece of toast, a bagel, or an English muffin. You can also spoon some into a tortilla shell, top with some nondairy cheese, and enjoy as a tasty breakfast burrito.

Tempting Tempeh Meatballs

Who doesn't love meatballs? These versatile little gems are meaty, tender, and delicious. They are great with pasta, in a sandwich, or chopped up and added to pizza.

1. Heat 2 tablespoons of the oil in a large skillet over medium-high heat. Add the onion, mushrooms, and ½ teaspoon of the salt. Sauté until the vegetables are tender and lightly browned.

2. Add the garlic and sauté for a minute, then add the tempeh. Continue cooking until the tempeh is heated through and beginning to brown, about 4 to 5 minutes.

3. Add the remaining ingredients, except the wheat gluten and broth, and stir to combine. Transfer to the bowl of a food processor and process until completely ground. Add the wheat gluten and broth. Pulse to combine into a dough-like consistency.

4. Wipe out the skillet used to cook the vegetables and heat the remaining 1 teaspoon of oil over medium-high heat. Taking approximately 2 tablespoons of the dough at a time, form into balls. Brown them in the skillet on each side, about 6 to 8 minutes, then reduce the heat to low and continue to cook for another 10 to 15 minutes or until firm.

Store in an airtight container in the refrigerator for up to 5 days.

Makes 30–36 meatballs.

Fun Fact: *Garlic is one of the oldest cultivated crops. It was fed to the builders of the Great Pyramid in Egypt in the belief that it gave them strength. Recent studies have found that freshly pressed garlic extract (even when highly diluted) reduced or killed a number of germs, including drug-resistant strains of bacteria. That same antibacterial substance in garlic (allicin) has been shown to protect cells from cancer-causing substances and slow the spread of cancer.*

2 tablespoons plus 1 teaspoon olive oil, divided
½ medium onion, chopped
10–12 cremini mushrooms, chopped
1½ teaspoons sea salt, divided
2 cloves garlic, minced
8 ounces tempeh, broken into small pieces
1 cup walnuts
1 tablespoon coconut aminos or tamari
1 teaspoon coconut crystals or other dry sweetener of your choice
½ teaspoon sage
½ teaspoon thyme
½ teaspoon black pepper
½ teaspoon marjoram
¼ teaspoon nutmeg
¼ teaspoon smoked paprika
¼ teaspoon red pepper flakes
½ teaspoon fennel seed, ground
¾ cup vital wheat gluten
¼ cup low-sodium vegetable broth

Crispy Baked Taquitos

The first time we made these for our family, we all ended up with burnt tongues from eating them so quickly. They were just so delicious, we couldn't wait for them to cool. While they are great on their own, they are even better when topped with Creamy Cashew Sauce. Enjoy!

1½ tablespoons olive oil or other neutral-flavor oil, divided

1 cup diced red onion

2 cloves garlic, minced

2 bean or vegetable burgers, crumbled (Pumpkin Hemp Seed Burger, Zucchini Almond Burger, Cheesy Burrito Burger, and Adzuki Bean Burger all work great)

1 large sweet potato, diced and oven-roasted (see Quick Tip below)

1¾ cups cooked black beans

½ cup sweet corn (thaw if frozen)

1 teaspoon cumin

½ teaspoon oregano

½ teaspoon coriander

½ teaspoon paprika

¼ teaspoon chili powder

1 tablespoon freshly squeezed lime juice

Sea salt to taste

10–12 flour tortillas of your choice, kept at room temperature 30 minutes before using (gluten-free if needed)

Creamy Cashew Sauce (optional topping; page 121)

1. Preheat the oven to 425°F. Line a baking sheet with parchment paper or nonstick foil and set aside.

2. Heat 1 tablespoon of the oil in a large sauté pan over medium-high heat. Add the onion and garlic and sauté until the onion is translucent.

3. Add the crumbled burgers, sweet potato, black beans, corn, cumin, oregano, coriander, paprika, chili powder, lime juice, and salt to the pan and continue to cook for another 2 to 3 minutes, stirring often.

4. Place the tortillas on a flat surface and evenly spoon the bean mixture onto the center of each tortilla. Roll the tortillas into a tube and place on the prepared baking sheet. Make sure to place the tortilla seam side down. Lightly brush the top of each tortilla with the remaining oil if desired, to give them a nice crunchy brown texture.

5. Bake the taquitos in the oven for 10 minutes or until golden brown. Remove and serve immediately with a side of Creamy Cashew Sauce.

Makes 10–12 taquitos.

Quick Tip: Here's a quick and easy method for roasting sweet potatoes. Preheat the oven to 375°F. Scrub the potato, dice, and place on a baking sheet. Drizzle with olive oil and a pinch of salt and bake for 35 to 40 minutes or until the edges are browned.

Fancy No-Quesa-Dilla

We feel that this meal would be right at home on the menu at a fancy, high-end restaurant. You know the kind of menu filled with weird-sounding dishes where you think, *No way is this going to be good,* and it turns out to be the best meal you've ever eaten? Now you don't have pay the high-end prices to experience the best quesadilla you've ever had.

1. Heat the oil in a large sauté pan over medium-high heat. Add the Brussels sprouts and garlic and cook for 2 to 3 minutes.

2. Add in the parsley, sea salt, and crumbled burger. Stir well and continue to cook until the sprouts are tender. Remove from the pan and set aside.

3. Spread the hummus evenly between 2 tortillas. Top with half of the sprout mixture, the Dijon mustard, and the remaining tortillas.

4. Transfer the quesadilla to a large nonstick sauté pan and cook over medium heat until each side is golden brown. Remove from the heat and let cool for 2 to 3 minutes before cutting into thirds and serving. If desired, serve with our Ranch Dressing (page 125) or Rockin' Creamy Almond Sauce (page 129) for dipping.

Makes 2 servings.

Quick Tip: When purchasing tortillas, look for brands that have these four simple ingredients: organic whole wheat, water, organic oil (usually canola, sunflower, or safflower), and salt.

1 tablespoon olive oil or other neutral-flavor oil

1½ cups shredded Brussels sprouts

1–2 cloves garlic, minced

1½ tablespoons freshly chopped parsley

1 teaspoon sea salt

1 good-sized bean or vegetable burger, crumbled (Greek Chicken Burger, Roasted Eggplant Patty, or Zucchini Almond Burger all work great)

¼ cup Creamy Roasted Garlic Hummus (page 120)

4 tortillas of your choice (10-inch size or larger)

2 tablespoons Dijon mustard

Nacho Cheese Taco Salad

One of our favorite uses for leftover bean and veggie burgers is a simple taco salad. This recipe is inspired from an old family recipe that unfortunately uses unhealthy, artificially flavored corn chips. With a few simple changes, we've refreshed this recipe for a more discerning palate!

3½ cups finely shredded lettuce

¾ cup diced tomato

1 small avocado, seeded, peeled, and diced

¼ cup diced red onion

2 tablespoons canola or other neutral-flavor oil

2 good-sized vegetable or bean burgers, crumbled (Cheesy Burrito Burgers, Spicy Chili Burgers, and Crunchy Burger Patties all work really well)

Heaping ½ cup finely crushed unseasoned tortilla chips of your choice

2 tablespoons Nacho Cheese Seasoning (recipe on page 184)

Ranch Dressing (page 125) or other dressing of your choice

1. Place the lettuce, tomato, avocado, and red onion in a large salad bowl and toss well. Set aside.

2. Heat the oil in a large sauté pan over medium-high heat. Add the crumbled burgers, crushed tortilla chips, and Nacho Cheese Seasoning to the pan and stir well. Let the mixture cook until well heated, about 5 to 7 minutes.

3. Remove from heat and transfer to the salad bowl. Toss the salad again and top with Ranch Dressing or another of your favorite salad dressings.

Makes 4 servings as a main dish or 8 servings as a side dish.

Quick Tip: Tortilla salad bowls are a creative and yummy way to serve up many of your favorite salads, including our Nacho Cheese Taco Salad. Coat an inverted bowl with cooking spray and place it on a baking sheet. Gently press the tortilla around the outside and bake in a preheated oven at 350°F for 3 to 5 minutes or until browned and crispy.

Nacho Cheese Seasoning

This recipe was inspired by a popular brand of artificially flavored nacho cheese corn chips. We've taken healthy ingredients and combined them to create a delicious seasoning mix that is ideal not only for our Nacho Cheese Taco Salad but also for sprinkling on roasted or baked potatoes, tossing with pasta, and mixing with your favorite popcorn.

6 tablespoons nutritional yeast

1 teaspoon onion powder

1 teaspoon garlic powder

⅛–¼ teaspoon cayenne

1 heaping teaspoon smoked paprika

½ teaspoon sea salt

¼ teaspoon yellow mustard powder

Quick Tip: Are you feeling like a little "Cool Ranch"? Simply omit the cayenne and paprika from the recipe and add in ½ teaspoon of parsley, 1 teaspoon of chives, and an additional ¼ teaspoon of garlic.

Place all the ingredients in a blender and pulse 2 or 3 times. Store any leftover seasoning mix in a sealed container in a cool, dry place.

Makes approximately ½ cup.

Meat Lover's Pizza

Saturday night is pizza night at our house, and this simple and easy recipe is by far the most requested. This meal is sure to please meat eaters and plant eaters alike.

1. Preheat the oven to 450°F.

2. Spread the pizza sauce evenly across the top of the pizza dough, leaving at least a ½-inch edge around the outside for the crust.

3. Sprinkle the cheese evenly over the top, followed by the crumbled burgers and sausages. Finish with a sprinkling of red pepper flakes if desired.

4. Place the pizza on a baking stone or straight onto the oven rack and bake for 8 to 10 minutes, or until the cheese is melted and the pizza is heated through.

Store wrapped in foil in the refrigerator for up to 2 days.

Makes 6–8 servings.

1 cup pizza sauce of your choice

1 10- to 12-inch pre-baked pizza crust of your choice (gluten-free if needed)

1½ cups shredded nondairy mozzarella cheese of your choice (or a combination of mozzarella and cheddar)

2 good-sized bean or vegetable burgers, crumbled (Zesty Bean Burgers, Pizza Burgers, Spicy Chili Burgers, Buffalo Black Bean Burgers, Caramelized Onion Burgers, Sweet Potato Quinoa Burgers, or another favorite burger)

2–3 Sun-Dried Tomato and Pepper Sausages or Roasted Garlic Hummus Dogs or a combination of both, cut into slices (omit for a gluten-free pizza)

1 tablespoon red pepper flakes (optional)

Quick Tip: Sautéed vegetables—such as onions, red peppers, garlic, zucchini, spinach, mushrooms, and black olives—are an excellent optional topping on your pizza.

185

Easy Shepherd's Pie

In the colder months, we love breaking into our stash of frozen bean and veggie burgers to make this classic comfort food. The hearty and tangy vegetable mixture pairs wonderfully with the creamy mashed potatoes. A perfect meal for enjoying by the fire with a glass of wine!

1. Preheat the oven to 350°F.

2. Place the potatoes in a large soup pot and add enough water to cover the potatoes. Bring to a boil, reduce heat, and simmer, covered, for 15 to 20 minutes or until easily pierced through with a fork.

3. Drain the water and transfer the potatoes to a large mixing bowl. Add the nondairy milk and the butter (if using). Using a potato masher or a handheld electric mixer, mash the potatoes until they are a smooth, creamy texture. Add in the sea salt and nutritional yeast and mix until thoroughly combined. Set aside.

4. In a large sauté pan, heat the oil over medium-high heat. Add the onion and garlic and cook until the onion is translucent.

5. Add the peas and carrots, crumbled burgers, tomato paste, soy sauce, Worcestershire sauce, and vegetable broth to the pan. Continue to cook for another 5 minutes or until the mixture is heated through.

6. Transfer the vegetable mixture to an oven-safe baking dish and top with the mashed potatoes. Use a spatula or the back of a spoon to make a smooth, even layer.

7. Bake in the oven for 30 minutes or until the top is golden brown. Remove from oven and serve immediately.

Store in an airtight container in the refrigerator for up to 3 days.

Makes 6–8 servings.

1 pound Yukon Gold potatoes, peeled and quartered

½ cup nondairy milk

2–3 tablespoons nondairy butter (optional)

1 teaspoon sea salt

3 tablespoons nutritional yeast

1–2 tablespoons olive oil or other neutral-flavor oil

½ cup diced yellow onion

1–2 cloves garlic, minced

2 cups frozen peas and carrots, thawed

2 cups crumbled bean or vegetable burgers of your choice (about 2–3 burgers)

6 ounces tomato paste

3 tablespoons soy sauce or tamari (gluten-free if needed)

2 tablespoons Worcestershire sauce (gluten-free if needed)

1 cup vegetable broth

Quick Tip: Add ½ cup each of sliced mushrooms and sweet corn during step 5 and continue as directed. The mushrooms add texture while the corn adds a hint of sweetness.

Chili Cheese Fries

We are big football fans, and Sunday night football is just not complete without a plate of chili cheese fries to share. While we love this chili sauce on top of some hot and crispy french fries, it's also delicious on a baked potato or a Roasted Garlic Hummus Dog (page 198).

1 tablespoon olive oil or other neutral-flavor oil

1 cup finely chopped onion

¼ teaspoon sea salt

2 cups finely chopped bean or vegetable burgers (Zesty Bean Burger, Pizza Burger, Crunchy Burger Patty, or Buffalo Black Bean Burger work great)

3 tablespoons prepared yellow mustard

¼ cup apple cider vinegar

1 tablespoon Worcestershire sauce (gluten-free if needed)

½ cup tomato sauce

½ cup ketchup

2–3 tablespoons hot sauce (optional)

Vegetable broth as needed

16 ounces cooked french fries (see Quick Tip)

1 cup nondairy shredded cheddar cheese

1. Heat the oil in a large sauté pan over medium-high heat. Add the onion and salt and sauté until the onion is translucent.

2. Add the chopped burgers, mustard, vinegar, Worcestershire sauce, tomato sauce, ketchup, and hot sauce (if using). Stir well.

3. Let the mixture simmer for about 5 minutes, adding in vegetable broth as needed to obtain the desired consistency (for a thinner chili sauce, add 1 or more cups of broth).

4. Remove the chili sauce from the heat and pour over the french fries. Top with cheese and serve while hot.

Makes 4 servings.

Quick Tip: For this recipe we recommend using store-bought frozen french fries. Make sure to check the ingredients label and stick with brands that use only organic potatoes, organic oil (usually canola or olive oil), and organic apple juice (used to promote browning).

Sun-Dried Tomato and Pepper Sausages

Hummus isn't just for pita chips. It makes a really great sausage, too. With just a few additional ingredients, hummus takes on a whole new look and becomes one of your favorite "hot dogs."

5 sun-dried tomatoes, soaked in ¾ cup hot water (reserve water for later use)

1 red pepper, roasted and skinned (see Quick Tip on page 195)

1 teaspoon capers

1½ cups Sun-Dried Tomato Hummus (page 120)

⅓ cup nutritional yeast

1 teaspoon basil

1 teaspoon oregano

1 teaspoon onion powder

½ teaspoon sea salt or to taste

½ teaspoon red pepper flakes (optional)

1 cup vital wheat gluten

1 tablespoon olive oil

1. Preheat a steamer according to the manufacturer's instructions. Set aside 14 to 16 foil sheets.

2. Place the sun-dried tomatoes, roasted red pepper, capers, and 2 tablespoons of the reserved water in the bowl of a food processor. Process until smooth.

3. Transfer the tomato mixture to a large bowl. Add the remaining ingredients except the vital wheat gluten and olive oil. Mix well.

4. Add the vital wheat gluten, and stir until a soft dough has formed. Add 1 to 2 tablespoons more of the reserved water if needed.

5. Take a plum-sized piece of dough and roll it into a 6-inch log. Place it along one edge of a foil sheet and roll it up, twisting the ends to seal. Repeat with the remaining dough.

6. Place the foil rolls in the steamer basket and steam for 45 minutes. Remove from the steamer and unwrap.

7. In a large skillet, heat the oil over medium-high heat. Cook the sausages for 4 to 5 minutes until nicely browned.

Store in an airtight container in the refrigerator for 3 to 4 days, or in a freezer-safe container in the freezer for 1 to 2 months.

Makes 14–16 sausages.

Quick Tip: If you don't have a steamer, don't fret! Fill a large pot with 2 to 3 inches of water. Bring to a simmer. Lay a metal colander (don't try it with plastic) over the top with the sausages inside (you will probably have to work in batches) and cover with the lid. Check the sausages after 45 minutes to see if they are firm; if not, continue steaming a little longer making sure that the water has not boiled out of the pot. Add more water if necessary.

Italian Meatball Sub

Sure, meatballs are great served with spaghetti, but they are even better when placed on a crusty piece of bread and topped with creamy ranch dressing, tasty pesto, and sautéed peppers and onions!

1 tablespoon olive oil

½ small yellow onion, thinly sliced

¼ red pepper, cut into thin slices

¼ yellow or orange pepper, cut into thin slices

Sprinkle of sea salt

2 tablespoons Pumpkin Seed Pesto (recipe on next page)

1 whole-grain sandwich bun of your choice, sliced and toasted if desired

6 Tempting Tempeh Meatballs (page 177)

4 tablespoons marinara sauce of your choice

2 tablespoons Ranch Dressing (page 125)

1. In a small sauté pan, heat the olive oil over medium heat. Add the onion and pepper, and sprinkle with sea salt. Cook, stirring occasionally, for 20 to 25 minutes or until soft and caramelized (lower the heat if the onions and peppers get too brown).

2. Spread an even layer of pesto on the top half of your sandwich bun. Place a row of meatballs on the bottom half of the bun and top with marinara sauce and ranch dressing.

3. Add the sautéed onions and peppers and replace the top bun.

Makes 1 sandwich.

Quick Tip: To make this sandwich easier to eat for younger kids, dice the tempeh meatballs and sautéed onions and peppers and mix with marinara sauce. Place the mixture on the bun and top with Ranch Dressing and Pumpkin Seed Pesto.

Pumpkin Seed Pesto

Most traditional pesto recipes call for pine nuts, an expensive and unnecessary option. We love the flavor that the pumpkin seeds bring to this pesto, and the addition of kale adds a healthy dose of vitamins and nutrients.

Place all of the ingredients in a blender or food processor and process for 20 to 30 seconds or until you have a smooth consistency, adding more oil if necessary.

Store in an airtight container in the refrigerator for up to 1 week.

Makes approximately 1½ cups.

1 cup fresh basil leaves, lightly packed

1¼ cups extra-virgin olive oil

½ cup pumpkin seeds, raw or roasted (choose roasted for a richer flavor)

2 cloves garlic

½ tablespoon sea salt (omit if using salted pumpkin seeds)

2 teaspoons freshly squeezed lemon juice

½ cup finely chopped kale

Fun Fact: Did you know that ½ cup of pumpkin seeds contains 20 grams of protein, which is about 40 percent of the daily recommended value? Pumpkin seeds have been shown to increase in nutritive value as they age. According to research done in the Massachusetts Agricultural Experimental Station, squash and the seeds of pumpkins that have been stored for a long, long time increase their protein content.

Classic Italian Lasagna

The fragrant, flavorful sauce filled with diced tempeh meatballs along with freshly made macadamia nut "ricotta" give this dish that classic look, taste, and texture you expect in a lasagna. Be sure to plan ahead when making this recipe as the nuts in the Macadamia Nut Ricotta Cheese need to soak overnight.

1. Preheat the oven to 350°F.

2. Heat a large skillet over medium-high heat. Add the oil, meatballs, onion, and salt. Cook until the onion is tender. Add the garlic and cook 1 to 2 minutes more. Add the crushed tomatoes, red pepper, basil, and oregano. Cover, reduce to a simmer, and let the pasta sauce cook for 10 minutes.

3. Spread ½ cup of the pasta sauce evenly over the bottom of an 11x7-inch baking pan. Place 2 cooked lasagna noodles side by side over the sauce. Spread ½ cup of the Macadamia Nut Ricotta Cheese evenly over the noodles. Layer ⅓ of the spinach over the ricotta. Spread 1 cup of sauce evenly over the spinach, then evenly sprinkle ½ cup of the mozzarella over the sauce. Repeat the same sequence for 2 more layers.

4. Cover with foil and bake for 30 minutes. Remove the foil and continue baking for 10 to 15 minutes or until hot and bubbly. Remove from the oven and let sit for 10 minutes before cutting.

Store in an airtight container in the refrigerator for up to 1 week.

Makes 6 servings.

Quick Tip: To roast a red pepper, begin by preheating your oven to 400°F. Line a baking sheet with nonstick foil and lay the pepper on its side on the foil. Roast in the oven for 20 minutes. Remove the baking sheet and, using a pair of tongs, turn the pepper over and then roast for an additional 20 minutes. After 20 minutes, the skin should be charred and soft, and the pepper should look slightly collapsed. If not, let it roast for a few more minutes. When the pepper is done, let it cool completely before skinning and seeding it.

2 tablespoons olive oil

6 Tempting Tempeh Meatballs (page 177), diced

½ cup diced onion

1 teaspoon salt

2 cloves garlic, minced

3 cups crushed tomatoes or tomato sauce

1 red pepper, roasted, skinned, seeded, and diced (or store-bought roasted peppers)

2 tablespoons basil

2 tablespoons oregano

6 whole-wheat or brown rice lasagna noodles, cooked al dente

1½ cups Macadamia Nut Ricotta Cheese (recipe on next page)

8 cups fresh baby spinach, steamed, or a 9- to 10-ounce package chopped frozen spinach, thawed and drained

1½ cups nondairy shredded mozzarella cheese

Macadamia Nut Ricotta Cheese

Heart-healthy macadamia nuts are the star of the show in this delicious plant-based ricotta cheese. We've featured this cheese in our Classic Italian Lasagna (page 195) but you can also use it as a topping for sliced baguettes, on a baked potato, tossed with your favorite salad, or added to pasta dishes for an extra creamy flavor.

1 cup raw macadamia or cashew nuts, soaked overnight

2 tablespoons nutritional yeast

2 tablespoons freshly squeezed lemon juice

1 teaspoon sea salt

¼ cup water

Place all of the ingredients in a high-powered blender. Process until creamy and smooth, tamping the ingredients down as necessary to blend them evenly. Add a little more water if necessary to get the desired consistency.

Store in an airtight container in the refrigerator for up to 5 days.

Makes approximately 1 cup.

Sausage and Jalapeño Corn Muffins

Sweet corn muffins with a jalapeño kick. This quick and easy recipe uses leftover Sun-Dried Tomato and Pepper Sausage to turn a good muffin into a golden treat.

1. Preheat the oven to 350°F. Grease or line a muffin pan with paper liners.

2. In a large bowl, combine the cornmeal, flour, soy milk powder, baking powder, tapioca starch, potato starch, and salt.

3. Add the soy milk, coconut oil, and maple syrup. Mix just until combined. Stir in the corn, jalapeño, sausage, and cheese.

4. Pour the mixture into the muffin cups about ¾ full. Bake in the oven for 20 to 25 minutes or until a toothpick inserted into the center comes out clean.

5. Let the muffins cool in the muffin pan for 5 minutes before removing to a plate or bowl.

Store at room temperature for 1 to 2 days in a tightly sealed container.

Makes 9 muffins.

1 cup cornmeal

½ cup white whole-wheat flour or whole-wheat pastry flour

2 tablespoons soy milk powder

1 tablespoon baking powder

1 tablespoon tapioca or corn starch

1 tablespoon potato starch

1 teaspoon sea salt

1 cup unsweetened soy milk, warmed

2 tablespoons coconut oil, melted

2 tablespoons maple syrup, coconut nectar, or honey

⅓ cup corn (fresh, canned, or thawed if frozen)

1 jalapeño, diced

1 Sun-Dried Tomato and Pepper Sausage, diced (page 190)

½ cup nondairy shredded cheddar cheese

Roasted Garlic Hummus Dogs

Roasted garlic and deli spices turn hummus into hot dogs. Chicago-style or with just plain ketchup, either way it's all good.

1 cup Creamy Roasted Garlic
   Hummus (page 120)
1 tablespoon coconut aminos
   (omit if not available)
1 tablespoon coconut crystals
   or other dry sweetener of
   your choice
2 teaspoons dry mustard
1–2 teaspoons smoked
   paprika
1 teaspoon sea salt
1 teaspoon sage
1 teaspoon thyme
1 teaspoon marjoram
½ teaspoon black pepper
¼ teaspoon nutmeg
2–4 tablespoons low-sodium
   vegetable broth
1 cup vital wheat gluten
1 tablespoon olive oil

1. Preheat a steamer according to the manufacturer's instructions. Set aside 12 foil sheets.

2. Place the hummus in a large bowl. Add the next 10 ingredients and 2 tablespoons of the broth. Mix well.

3. Add in the vital wheat gluten and stir until a soft dough forms. Add the remaining broth if the dough appears too dry.

4. Take a plum-sized portion of the dough and roll it into a 6-inch log. Place it along the edge of a foil sheet and roll it up. Twist the ends closed. Complete the same process with the remaining dough.

5. Place the hummus dogs in the steamer basket and steam for 45 minutes. Remove and unwrap.

6. In a large skillet, heat the oil over medium heat. Add the sausages and cook for 4 to 5 minutes, turning to brown on all sides.

Store in an airtight container in the refrigerator for 3 to 4 days, or in a freezer-safe container in the freezer for 1 to 2 months.

Makes 8–10 hummus dogs.

Quick Tip: Roasted Garlic Hummus Dogs are fantastic for packing in lunches. Because they don't contain meat, you can warm them up and not worry about E. coli or salmonella. Simply warm a hummus dog up in the microwave, oven, or on the stove and wrap securely in tin foil, making sure to seal the ends tightly. The hummus dogs will stay warm for 4 to 5 hours.

Sizzlin' Satay

When making satay, it's all about the marinade, and this marinade is sizzlin' good.

1. Place all of the ingredients except the hummus dogs and rice into a saucepan and heat over medium-low heat. Heat until the sauce is smooth and the coconut crystals are dissolved, about 3 to 5 minutes. Remove from heat and let cool.

2. Pour half of the sauce into a bowl or a ziplock bag and add the hummus dogs. Let them marinate for about 10 to 15 minutes. Set aside the other half of the sauce.

3. Preheat an outdoor grill or indoor grill pan. Rub with a little oil to prevent sticking. Thread the marinaded hummus dogs onto the skewers. Grill on each side for 1 to 2 minutes or until they have nicely colored grill marks.

4. Serve over rice (if using) with the reserved sauce.

Makes 4–6 skewers.

Quick Tip: If using bamboo skewers, it's best to soak them for about 30 minutes before use to avoid having them burn on the grill.

¾ cup no-salt-added peanut butter
½ cup soy sauce or tamari
½ cup coconut water
¼ cup coconut butter
2 cloves garlic, chopped
1 inch fresh ginger, peeled and chopped
Zest (about 1 teaspoon) and juice (about 3 tablespoons) of 1 lemon
4 tablespoons coconut crystals or other dry sweetener of your choice
1 teaspoon tamarind paste
2 teaspoons ground coriander
2 teaspoons red pepper flakes
8 Roasted Garlic Hummus Dogs, cut into 1-inch chunks (page 198)
2 cups cooked rice (optional)

Stuffed Eggplant

These stuffed eggplants are filled with pepper, tomato, spinach, and last night's leftover Mushroom and Lentil Burgers, making leftovers a cause for celebration.

1 large eggplant, leaves removed but stem intact

2½ teaspoons salt, divided

2 tablespoons olive oil

1 red pepper, diced

1 large tomato, diced

1 cup spinach, chopped

½ teaspoon thyme

2 Mushroom and Lentil Burgers, chopped into ½-inch pieces (page 39)

1. Cut the eggplant in half lengthwise. Using a small paring knife, cut down the center of the eggplant halves, being careful not to pierce the skin. Then run the knife along the inside edge, again without piercing the skin. Using a spoon, scoop out the flesh and dice.

2. Sprinkle ½ teaspoon of the salt evenly over the inside of the eggplant shells. Sprinkle 1½ teaspoons of the salt over the diced eggplant and place them in a colander for 30 minutes. Thoroughly rinse both the eggplant shells and diced pieces and pat dry. Place the eggplant shells in an oven-proof baking dish and set aside.

3. Preheat the oven to 350°F. Heat a skillet over medium-high heat. Add the oil, diced eggplant, red pepper, and remaining ½ teaspoon of salt. Cook until softened, about 5 minutes.

4. Add the tomato, spinach, and thyme. Cook until the spinach has wilted, about 2 to 3 minutes. Gently stir in the chopped burger. Spoon the mixture into the eggplant shells.

Bake for 30 minutes or until hot and steamy.

Makes 4 servings.

Quick Tip: If you find yourself without a veggie burger on hand and still want to make a Beyond Burger recipe, try substituting it with crumbled tempeh instead. Use a hand chopper or a knife to chop the tempeh into small crumbles. Add to a nonstick sauté pan and cook until slightly crispy and heated through, approximately 5 minutes. Note: ½ cup of cooked tempeh is equal to one bean or vegetable burger.

Soul Bowl

Soul Bowl /sōl bōl/ noun: the ultimate comfort food. That's our definition of it, anyway. Whip up a bowl and nourish both mind and body one delicious spoonful at a time.

1. Place the carrot and zucchini in a saucepan with a tight-fitting lid. Add about ½ cup of water, or just enough to fill the saucepan to a depth of 1 inch.

2. Cover the saucepan and bring the water to a boil. Let the vegetables steam for about 3 to 5 minutes or until tender when pierced with a fork. Add the kale and steam for 1 minute more.

3. Remove the vegetables and place in a bowl with the rice, beans, and crumbled burger pieces. Top with the ranch dressing and BBQ sauce. Serve immediately.

Makes 1 serving.

Quick Tip: *This meal is also fantastic when served as a "soul wrap." Place the rice, veggies, beans, and crumbled burger on a tortilla shell and top with Ranch Dressing and BBQ sauce. Roll up the tortilla and enjoy!*

1 small carrot, diced
1 small zucchini, diced
3–4 leaves of kale, stems removed and roughly chopped
1 cup cooked brown rice
1 cup cooked kidney beans
1 crumbled bean or vegetable burger (Zesty Bean Burger, Cheesy Burrito Burger, Thin and Crispy "Chicken Sandwich" Burger, and Crunchy Burger Patties all work great)
2 tablespoons Ranch Dressing (page 125)
2 tablespoons Sweet and Tangy BBQ Sauce (page 119)

Asian Lettuce Wraps

These easy wraps are a great way to use leftover burgers for those busy days when you need a tasty meal in a hurry.

¼ cup soy sauce or tamari (gluten-free if needed)

3 tablespoons brown rice vinegar

2 tablespoons peanut oil

1 teaspoon toasted sesame oil

1 tablespoon coconut nectar, honey, or brown rice syrup

1 teaspoon granulated garlic

1 teaspoon ground ginger

¼ teaspoon red pepper flakes

2 cups shredded Napa cabbage

1 cup shredded bok choy

2 green onions, thinly sliced

1 carrot, grated

½ red bell pepper, thinly sliced

4 burgers of your choice (Pad Thai Burger, Miso Ginger Mung Bean Burger, Asian Quinoa Burger, Asian Corn Burger, and Happy Crabby Patty all work great)

8 leaves lettuce (butterhead lettuce, leaf lettuce, or romaine)

1. In a small bowl, whisk together the soy sauce, vinegar, peanut oil, sesame oil, coconut nectar, garlic, ginger, and red pepper flakes.

2. In a large bowl, toss together the cabbage, bok choy, green onions, carrot, red bell pepper, and half of the dressing from Step 1. Set aside while preparing the remaining ingredients.

3. Roughly chop the burgers and place in a dry nonstick skillet over medium heat. Cook 3 to 4 minutes, stirring occasionally until warmed through.

4. Divide the chopped burgers evenly between the lettuce leaves and top each one with a spoonful of the cabbage mixture.

5. Serve the remaining dressing as a dipping sauce for the lettuce wraps.

Makes 4 servings.

Fun Fact: Napa cabbage, along with bok choy, is one of the popular cabbage vegetables in China. Napa's sweet, crunchy leaves make an ideal ingredient for salads, sandwiches, soups, stir-fries, and burgers. Napa cabbage is loaded with antioxidants, folates, vitamin C, and vitamin K, and is a wonderful source of fiber.

BEVERAGES

Root Beer Float with Homemade Ice Cream

Root beer floats are a favorite childhood treat that we can enjoy just as much as adults. Homemade ice cream really takes this drink to a whole new level.

28 ounces full-fat coconut milk

⅓–½ cup coconut nectar, honey, or other liquid sweetener of your choice

2–3 tablespoons vanilla extract or vanilla powder

Root beer beverage of your choice

1. In a large bowl, mix together the coconut milk, ⅓ cup of coconut nectar, and 2 tablespoons of vanilla extract. Give the mixture a taste and add in the additional coconut nectar and vanilla if you'd like a sweeter ice cream with a more pronounced vanilla flavor.

2. Transfer the mixture to an ice cream maker and follow the manufacturer's instructions to finish preparing your ice cream. If you don't have an ice cream maker, transfer the mixture to a 9 x 13-inch glass baking dish and place directly in the freezer. Stir with a fork every 30 minutes or so to break up the edges that freeze faster than the middle. Freeze until the ice cream has a soft-serve consistency (the length of time will depend on your freezer setting).

3. Spoon a scoop or two of ice cream into a tall glass. Slowly pour root beer into the glass, allowing the foam to rise and then recede before adding more root beer.

Makes approximately 4 cups of ice cream.

Quick Tip: *Using an alcohol-based vanilla extract will keep the ice cream from getting too hard once it's placed in the freezer for storage. It can be stored for up to 6 months.*

Fruity Sangria Punch

This is one of our favorite beverages to serve whenever we host a party or get-together. With or without alcohol, it's a sure crowd pleaser.

1 large apple, cored and
    diced
1 large orange, peeled or
    unpeeled and diced
1 lime, diced
1 cup halved strawberries
½ cup diced pineapple
½ cup pineapple juice
1 cup cranberry juice
1 cup pomegranate juice
25 ounces sparkling water or
    your favorite red wine

Quick Tip: When purchasing fruit juice, be sure to read the label and look for no added sugars or sweeteners. Remember, organic is always best when it comes to fruit juice.

1. Combine all the ingredients (except the sparkling water if using) in a large pitcher and place in the fridge for at least 12 hours before serving. If using sparking water, add right before you are ready to serve.

2. Pour the sangria over ice and garnish with some of the marinated fruit.

Makes approximately 5 cups.

Pineapple Sunshine Cooler

No matter where you live or what the weather is like, this drink will make you feel like you're in the tropics on a beautiful sunny beach. It's like sunshine in a glass!

Place the first 3 ingredients in a blender and process until smooth. Pour over crushed ice or add the ice to the blender and pulse once or twice to mix.

Makes 2 servings.

3 cups diced ripe pineapple
1 large orange, peeled
½ banana, peeled
Crushed ice

Strawberry Lemonade

We just love the tangy lemon mixed with super-sweet summer strawberries in this lemonade. It's like summer poured into a glass.

2 cups cold water

1 quart fresh ripe
    strawberries, hulled

¾ cup coconut crystals,
    coconut nectar, or honey

¾ cup freshly squeezed
    lemon juice

2 cups sparkling water

1. Place half of the cold water, half of the strawberries, and half of the coconut crystals in a blender and process until smooth. Transfer to a large pitcher and repeat with the remaining water, strawberries, and coconut crystals.

2. Stir in the lemon juice and sparkling water. Serve immediately and garnish with lemon wedges or strawberries if desired.

Makes approximately 2 quarts.

Quick Tip: For a bit of summer fun, pour your Strawberry Lemonade into popsicle molds and place in the freezer until frozen all the way through. You can also create a refreshing sorbet by filling a freezer-safe ziplock bag halfway with the liquid. Lay on a flat surface in the freezer and every 10 to 15 minutes, for approximately 2 hours, squeeze the bag to break up the chunks as it starts to freeze. Squeeze the sorbet from the bag into a bowl and serve.

Orange Coconut Cream

Lucuma or "eggfruit" is an exotic fruit native to the Peruvian Andes. It has a caramel or maple-like flavor. When lucuma powder is added to drinks, it not only sweetens them but creates a frothy texture. It's the perfect complement to fresh orange juice and coconut milk.

1. To cut open the coconut, you will need to make 4 cuts. Make the first cut by striking hard at the top of the coconut to cut all the way through the shell, not just the outer fiber. Make 3 more cuts to form a square. If you have cut all the way through, you should be able to remove the square.

2. Carefully pour the water in a bowl and then scrape out the inner white meat, taking care not to get any of the hard shell. There should be at least 1 cup of water and about ½ cup of meat.

3. Place the coconut water and meat in a blender and blend until smooth. Add the orange juice and lucuma powder, and blend until frothy. Pour into 4 glasses and sprinkle with cardamom powder if using.

Makes 4 servings.

1 young Thai coconut (or 1 cup canned coconut milk)
3 cups freshly squeezed orange juice, chilled
4 tablespoons lucuma powder
Pinch of cardamom powder (optional)

Quick Tip: If you can't find lucuma powder, you can substitute for it with 2 tablespoons of maple syrup and 2 tablespoons of soy milk powder.

Sparkling Raspberry Lemon Saki-tail

While beer is often the beverage of choice to go with a burger, a cocktail can fit right in too, and even elevate a meal, especially one as sparkling fresh as this beauty.

2 tablespoons freshly
  squeezed lemon juice
2 tablespoons coconut nectar
  or honey
1 tablespoon lemon zest
1 cup fresh raspberries
  (frozen can also be used)
10 ounces sparkling saki (or
  any sparkling white wine),
  chilled

Quick Tip: If you have lemongrass available, you can cut it into pieces to act as a natural swizzle stick. Instead of blending the saki with the raspberry mixture in the blender, simply pour equal amounts of each in a glass and serve with a stalk of lemongrass.

1. Combine the lemon juice and coconut nectar in a small saucepan and bring to a simmer over medium heat. Remove from heat and stir in the lemon zest. Let cool.

2. Place the raspberries and the lemon mixture in a blender and process until smooth. Pour in the saki and give a quick mix just to blend. Pour into glasses and serve.

Makes 4 servings.

Red Rooster

Sometimes when you're serving an amazing burger, plain old beer won't cut it. Similar to a Bloody Mary, this drink will complement any burger meal.

In a pitcher or large jar, combine all of the ingredients except the beer and celery sticks. Pour into 2 large glasses or mugs. Divide the beer evenly between the glasses and stir with the celery stalks.

Makes 2 servings.

- 1 cup tomato juice, chilled
- 2 tablespoons lime juice
- ½ teaspoon Worcestershire sauce (gluten-free if needed)
- 1 teaspoon hot sauce, more or less to taste
- ½ teaspoon sea salt
- ¼ teaspoon black pepper
- 1 cup very cold beer of your choice (gluten-free if needed)
- 2 celery stalks

Quick Tip: If you follow a strict vegetarian or vegan diet, you may be surprised to find out your favorite beer or wine isn't as veggie-friendly as you think. Many beers and wines are refined using a product called isinglass, which comes from fish, or may be filtered with bone char. For a list of vegetarian and vegan-friendly beers, visit www.peta.org or www.barnivore.com.

Ginger Watermelon Agua Fresca

Aguas frescas is Spanish for "fresh waters," and what could be fresher than watermelon, mint, and lime fizzed up with a little ginger ale?

4 cups cubed watermelon

¼ cup freshly squeezed lime juice (2–3 limes)

8–12 mint leaves, plus a couple to garnish

1 cup ginger ale beverage of your choice

1. Place the watermelon, lime juice, and 8 mint leaves in a blender. Blend until the mint is completely broken up and the liquid is slightly foamy.

2. Test to see if there is enough mint flavor and add more if desired. Blend again if additional mint is added.

3. Add the ginger ale and blend for just 1 to 2 seconds to mix. Pour into four glasses over ice and add mint to garnish.

Makes 4 servings.

Fun Fact: The most nutritious and delicious watermelons are the smaller, fully ripe ones with dark-red flesh. A red-ripe melon can have up to 3 times more lycopene (which reduces the incidence of cancer, cardiovascular disease, and macular degeneration) than a pale, semi-ripe melon. Look at the "ground spot," the area that was in contact with the soil. It should be yellow, not green or white. When you tap the watermelon, listen for a hollow sound rather than a flat thump. Unlike other fruit, watermelon will increase its antioxidant value after being harvested, provided it's not refrigerated. Keep melon on your counter for several days before cutting and chill before serving.

Iced Peach and Raspberry Chai

This drink is pretty to look at but even better to taste. The aromatic spiced tea blends beautifully with sweet peaches and a swirl of red raspberries to soothe away all the cares of the day.

1. Bring the water to a boil. Add the tea bags and steep for 15 minutes.

2. Stir in the coconut nectar, and place the tea in the refrigerator to chill.

3. Place the peaches in a blender along with the cooled tea. Blend until smooth.

4. Pour into 2 glasses. Divide the sparkling water evenly between the glasses and stir.

5. Place the raspberries in the blender and blend until smooth. Spoon half into each glass and stir gently with a swizzle stick or a skewer to swirl the beautiful red color into the drink.

Makes 2 servings.

1 cup water

2 chai-flavor tea bags

4 teaspoons coconut nectar
   or honey

4 peaches or nectarines,
   pitted and roughly
   chopped (peel if desired)

½ cup unflavored sparkling
   water, chilled

¼ cup fresh or frozen
   raspberries (thaw if frozen)

Refreshing Melon Cooler

Sweet melon, spicy ginger, and sparkling wine make this cooler a refreshing part of any meal. Or serve it as a drinkable after-dinner dessert.

¼ cup water

¼ cup coconut nectar or honey

½ teaspoon freshly ground ginger

2 limes

1 average-size honeydew melon, cut into pieces

½ cup sparkling white wine or unsweetened lime-flavored sparkling water, chilled

1. In a small saucepan, combine the water, coconut nectar, and ginger. Sauté over low heat until the nectar is completely dissolved. Remove the ginger water from the heat and chill in the refrigerator.

2. Zest one lime and set the zest aside. Squeeze the juice from the lime into a blender. Add the melon pieces and the chilled ginger water to the blender and blend until smooth.

3. Pour the melon drink into glasses. Stir in the lime zest and the white wine or sparkling water, and serve with slices of the remaining lime.

Makes 4 servings.

Quick Tip: When choosing a melon, look at the stem end. The fruit should have a slight depression. If it has a bit of a stub, it was probably picked while still green and won't have had time to develop its full flavor. Smell the stem end of the melon. A nicely ripe melon will have a sweet scent. If you lightly press the opposite end with your thumb, it should depress slightly.

Acknowledgments

This book, and everything that has led up to its creation, was inspired by the wonderful memories we share of our family's backyard barbecues. Many of these recipes are tried and true favorites that have been requested many times over at our get-togethers.

Our biggest thank you goes to Cliff, Caleb, and Keegan. Our sincerest appreciation for being the best taste testers anyone could ask for! We're sorry we made you eat veggie burgers for just about every meal for months on end.

We'd also like to thank our many friends and family members whose suggestions assisted in the design of many of our recipes. Your input and critiques helped shape each and every one.

Our sincere gratitude and many thanks goes to our publisher, Lyons Press, for giving us the opportunity to see our vision come to life. This book wouldn't be what it is today without the help of our amazing editor, Anna Bliss—thank you so much for all your help and insights. You've taught us so much and helped shape this book into so much more than we ever thought possible.

And lastly, we thank all our readers and friends in the blogging community. You inspire us every day and we thank you for your loyalty and support.

Index

About the Authors

Sarah Davies is a successful plant-based chef who loves helping people change their lives through healthy cooking, lectures, classes, and chef services. With her plant-based nutrition certification from e-Cornell, as well as other nutritional certifications, she works with groups and individuals to create delicious recipes and meals that even the pickiest of eaters will enjoy.

Sarah lives in Southern California with her husband, Cliff, and three children, Caleb, Keegan, and Madelyn. She enjoys homeschooling her children, spending time outdoors, and traveling. She will be completing her chef's training in raw foods and plans to produce more cookbooks during her culinary journey.

Kristy Taylor has been eating healthfully for many years to "feed" her running habit, but as she learned more about nutrition, she gradually adapted her diet to include completely unprocessed, unrefined, whole-food, plant-based fare. She has been cooking for her family, friends, and community for over thirty years. She enjoys everything about food, from the beauty of its colorful palette to its diverse tastes and textures. She delights in finding new ways to combine and cook ingredients to bring out the best from them.

Kristy lives in Southern California with her dog, Leo, and loves taking advantage of the beautiful weather year-round. She enjoys spending time with her grandchildren and helping her daughter, Sarah, in The Naked Kitchen.